Money Laundering

Money Laundering

A Concise Guide for All Business

DOUG HOPTON

GOWER

Published by
Gower Publishing Limited
Gower House
Croft Road
Aldershot
Hampshire GU11 3HR
England

Gower Publishing Company
Suite 420
101 Cherry Street
Burlington, VT 05401-4405
USA

Doug Hopton has asserted his moral right under the Copyright, Designs and Patents Act, 1988, to be identified as the author of this work.

British Library Cataloguing in Publication Data
Hopton, Doug
    Money laundering: a concise guide for all business
    1. Money laundering – Great Britain 2. Money Laundering
    3. Money laundering – Great Britain – Prevention 4. Money
    laundering – Prevention
    I. Title
    345.4'1'0268

    ISBN: 0 566 08639 5

Library of Congress Cataloging-in-Publication Data
Hopton, Doug.
    Money laundering: a concise guide for all business / Doug Hopton.
        p. cm.
    ISBN 0-566-08639-5
        1. Money laundering. I. Title.

    HV6768.H66 2005
    364.16'8--dc22

                                                                        2005057074

Printed and bound in Great Britain by MPG Books Ltd. Bodmin, Cornwall.

Contents

CHAPTER 1

Introduction to Money Laundering

There have been many books written in recent years on the subject of money laundering. There have been so many that one may easily forget that although, as a concept, money laundering has existed since the days of Prohibition in the USA, the fight against it, as we now understand it, has had a relatively short history. However, even over this short history the definition and meaning of money laundering has changed. This book, while considering the rationale of money laundering and its modern definition, will look not only at the current legislation and regulations, but also at some of the practical difficulties they impose and ways of overcoming these. However, to achieve this we must not only understand money laundering and the reasons for it but also understand the current laws, regulations and practice, particularly in the context of the United Kingdom. It will therefore be necessary to trace the history of money laundering both in the UK and internationally.

Money laundering has traditionally been considered to be a process by which criminals attempt to hide the origins and ownership of the proceeds of their criminal activities. The aim is to enable them to retain control over the proceeds and to provide, ultimately, a cover for their income and wealth. This has led people to believe that money laundering can be described in one of the following ways:

- turning dirty money into clean money
- washing drug money
- disguising criminal money.

These historical descriptions are fine as far as they go, but the actual term 'money laundering' is itself a misnomer. It does not recognise that in the modern world undertaking a laundering operation does not have to involve actual money. Consequently a modern definition would be that money laundering occurs every time any transaction takes place or relationship is formed which involves any form of property or benefit, whether it is tangible or intangible, which is derived from criminal activity. One must also not overlook the fact that you do not have to actually move the criminal proceeds to launder them. This is an aspect that can leave financial institutions, particularly banks, in a vulnerable position. The classic example would be in a case of tax evasion. Money earned for a legitimate activity is placed directly into a bank account in another country. At this point there is no problem as the money is legitimate. However, if the account holder fails to declare this income on a tax return in the country in which it was earned, the funds then become the proceeds of crime and the bank, although it may be unaware of it, is laundering the funds. Another traditional view of why money laundering is undertaken is that the criminals' objectives are the avoidance of detection, prosecution and confiscation of their ill-gotten gains. Now while in many cases this is true, there are cases that demonstrate that criminals' primary objective is not the conversion of property but the need to disguise the fact that they own the property. In doing so they break the connection between themselves and any property that can otherwise link them to the criminal offence for which they are seeking to avoid detection. Money laundering is therefore as much about disguising the ownership of property as it is about converting or washing criminal property. This clearly shows that even in a relationship where there is no obvious process by which money is received or paid away, money laundering can still occur.

THE MONEY LAUNDERING PROCESS

Obviously there is no one way of laundering money or other property. It can range from the simple method of using it in the form in which it is acquired to highly complex schemes involving a web of international businesses and investments.

Traditionally it has been accepted that the money laundering process comprises three stages:

- Placement – placing the criminal funds into the financial system directly or indirectly.

- Layering – the process of separating criminal proceeds from their source by using complex layers of financial transactions designed to hide the audit trail and provide anonymity.

- Integration – if the layering process succeeds, integration schemes place the laundered proceeds back into the legitimate economy in such a way that they appear to be normal business funds.

These stages, while they can be separate and distinct, more often occur simultaneously or overlap. It all depends on the facilities of the launderer, the requirements of the criminals, and on the robustness, or otherwise, of the regulatory and legal requirements linked to the effectiveness of the monitoring systems of the financial or regulated sector. However, this three-stage model, while a convenient way of describing the activity, is a little simplistic and does not fully reflect what really happens. It relates back to the common historical definition of money laundering discussed earlier. While they are examples of money laundering, they do not define what money laundering actually is. This has led to those with the duty of recognising money laundering having insufficient knowledge to be able to identify it in all its guises. Too often we have looked at money laundering from the aspect of what we expect it to look like, rather than by reference to what it actually is. Numerous cases have come to light where employees have failed to identify relationships in which property has been laundered, simply because what happened did not match with what they had been taught to expect such activity to look like. So while the traditional model is useful, it does not adequately cover all situations in which money laundering occurs.

Let us consider the following simple example.

> X is the beneficial owner of a Guernsey company (G) administered by a local corporate service provider. The company owns shares in another company, Y. X, acting on inside information regarding company Y, requests the corporate service provider to sell the shares owned by G. It does so.

The question is, has the corporate service provider assisted in the laundering of property? The simple answer is yes. However, this scenario does not fit into a traditional three-stage model since there is no placement, no layering and, so far, no attempt at integration.

So having considered this historical and traditional view of money laundering and the changes which have taken place, it leads us to recognise that this is a major international problem and not restricted to one country. Therefore, we now need to view this on an international basis and examine the efforts and actions that have been taken to combat it by the international community over the years. However, when examining the various actions against what I will call 'normal' money laundering, we must also consider terrorism and terrorist financing. This has become of greater importance across the world since the events of 11 September 2001 and subsequent terrorist actions.

TERRORISM AND TERRORIST FINANCING

Terrorist financing is considered by many to be just part of money laundering. To some extent this is correct, but it does have its own special aspects. First we will look at what we mean by terrorism. The International Convention for the Suppression of the Financing of Terrorism adopted by the United Nations General Assembly in December 1999 defines the primary objective of terrorism as 'to intimidate a population, or to compel a government or an international organisation to do or abstain from doing any act'. As can be seen, this is different from other forms of criminal activity where obtaining financial gain is often the ultimate objective. However, despite these different objectives, terrorist organisations, like other criminals, require financial help and support.

Terrorist organisations require finance for all aspects of their aims including training, materials and travel, so it is vital to them that they have an international flow of funds which they can use for their aims. It must be remembered that while the overall funds required by a terrorist organisation may be large, the cost of a particular 'attack' can be relatively small. The US authorities have, for example, estimated that the total cost of planning and carrying out the September 11 attacks in America at under US$300 000. The 1993 Bishopsgate Bomb in the City of London which caused loss of life as well as damage to property in excess of £1 billion has been estimated by the UK authorities to have only cost approximately £3000.

So how do terrorists raise the funds they need? Many different methods are used, but they generally fall into one of two categories:

- funds from supporter states or organisations;
- fund-raising either from legitimate or illegitimate sources.

Some examples of the second category are donations, charities and fund-raising, people-smuggling, drug trafficking, kidnapping and extortion or any other criminal activities. Recognising terrorist financing is, however, not easy, particularly in view of the small amounts frequently involved. This is discussed in detail in Chapter 14.

Having looked at money laundering and terrorist financing in general we will, over the next few chapters, examine the international initiatives and the UK legal and regulatory requirements. We will then go on to discuss practicalities, and problems of meeting these requirements.

CHAPTER 2

International Development of Law and Regulation

Having accepted the international breadth of the problem, let us now look at the actions taken by the international community. It is necessary to fully understand international historical efforts if we are to be able to fully interpret the current laws and regulations in force.

In recent years, increasing efforts have been made through trans-national organisations to reduce international, national and regional vulnerabilities and to take action against crime and corruption. The will of national governments to introduce effective anti-money laundering and terrorist financing strategies and to eradicate all forms of criminal finance and official corruption is increasingly being taken into account when considering the level of international aid to those countries. Countries that are unwilling to introduce and adopt international standards are finding their economic development being adversely affected as they suffer from a lack of international acceptance and co-operation. They are also suffering adverse publicity and finding that financial institutions around the world are being required to apply close scrutiny to transactions with them.[1] Sometimes an entire region can be affected and this is when the need for national and regional initiatives becomes vital. A number of countries, including the UK, can and do prohibit or restrict dealings with countries whose strategies to combat money laundering and terrorist financing are considered to be totally inadequate. The most obvious way is through the Non-Co-operative Countries and Territories list issued by the Financial Action Task Force (FATF), which is discussed in Chapter 3.

As part of the overall strategy, a number of initiatives have been developed both at national and international levels. Four tools are required for national action against money laundering to be effective:

1. The country's criminal justice system must be able to enforce effective tracing, freezing and eventually confiscation of the proceeds of criminal activity.

2. Legislation must be enacted and implemented to both criminalise

---

1   FATF Recommendation 21.

and counter the process of money laundering and terrorism financing.

3.   It is essential to recognise the need for an enhanced level of international co-operation, given the trans-national nature of the drugs trade and the sophisticated use made of the global financial system by the international traffickers to launder their funds and protect them from confiscation.

4.   The need to recognise that the criminal justice system cannot succeed alone. There is a need to establish legislation and regulation to empower and encourage the domestic and international financial sectors and professions to become partners in this task.

At the international level, there are now formal treaty-based mechanisms providing explicitly for coordinated action against money laundering. However, such treaties did not exist until the late 1980s. We will now examine these mechanisms and see how they have developed and enhanced international action against money laundering and terrorist financing.

FINANCIAL ACTION TASK FORCE (FATF)

This independent international body was established in 1989 at the Organisation for Economic Co-operation and Development (OECD) economic summit held in Paris. Its purpose is to develop and promote national and international strategies to combat money laundering. As a policy-making body, it attempts to generate the necessary political will to bring about national legislative and regulatory reforms to combat money laundering.

FATF has had a profound effect on both national laws and the international fight against money laundering, and this is fully discussed in Chapter 3.

EUROPEAN UNION

The European Union (EU) has issued two Directives on the Prevention of the Use of the Financial System for the Purpose of Money Laundering and is currently discussing a third. These Directives, which have a major impact on the laws and regulations against money laundering across the whole EU, are fully discussed in Chapter 4.

VIENNA CONVENTION

The United Nations Conference for the Adoption of a Convention Against Illicit Traffic in Narcotic Drugs and Psychotropic Substances was convened in Vienna in 1988. The scope of the Convention was restricted to drug-related money laundering although all countries were encouraged to extend their anti-money laundering measures to encompass all serious crimes. Article III of the Convention provided a comprehensive definition of money laundering, which has been the basis of virtually all subsequent legislation. This Convention, at the time, provided a significant step forward in the international fight against money laundering and made money laundering an internationally extraditable offence.

The Convention, which was ratified by more than 100 countries, came into effect in November 1990 and contained strict obligations on those countries that became parties to it:

- Criminalisation of drug trafficking and associated money laundering.

- To enact measures for the confiscation of the proceeds of drug trafficking.

- To enact measures to permit international assistance.

- To empower the courts to order bank, financial or commercial records to be made available to the enforcement agencies, notwithstanding any bank secrecy laws.

While the Vienna Convention formed the basis of much subsequent legislation, it has now effectively been overtaken by the Palermo Convention.

PALERMO CONVENTION

At its Millennium meeting in November 2000 the General Assembly of the United Nations adopted the United Nations Convention Against Trans-national Organised Crime. This Convention was opened for signature at a high-level conference held in Palermo, Italy in December 2002. It is significant in that it is the first legally binding UN instrument in the field of organised and serious crime. At the meeting in Italy 184 member countries signed the Treaty which would enter into force when 40 countries had ratified it.

The signatories are required to establish within their national laws the following four distinct criminal offences:

- participation in an organised criminal group

- money laundering

- corruption

- obstruction of justice.

The Convention also set out indications of how countries could improve co-operation on such matters as extradition, mutual legal assistance, transfer of proceedings and joint investigations. The signatories are also required to commit to providing technical assistance to developing countries to assist them in taking measures to deal with organised crime.

BASEL COMMITTEE ON BANKING REGULATIONS AND SUPERVISORY PRACTICE

The Basel Committee was established in 1974 by the governors of the central banks of the Group of ten countries. The membership of the committee as of October 2005 is made up of representatives from Belgium, Canada, France, Germany, Italy, Japan, Luxembourg, the Netherlands, Spain, Sweden, Switzerland, the UK and the USA. The committee meets regularly and has issued a number of papers in the fight against money laundering.

BASEL PRINCIPLES AND CUSTOMER DUE DILIGENCE FOR BANKS

In recognition of the vulnerability of the financial sector to misuse by criminals, the Basel Committee on Banking Regulations and Supervisory Practices issued a Statement of Principles (the 'Basel Principles') in December 1988. This was a significant step towards preventing the use of the banking sector for money laundering purposes, as it set out a number of major principles with which all banking institutions should comply in respect of:

- customer identification;

- compliance with legislation;

- conformity with high ethical standards and local laws and regulations;

- full co-operation with national law enforcement authorities to the extent permitted without breaching customer confidentiality;

- record-keeping and systems;

- staff training.

The Basel Principles stress co-operation within the confines of the duties of client confidentiality. This is understandable as they were issued before most countries enacted their current money-laundering legislation. This legislation provides for the disclosure of client information to law enforcement agencies and protection from civil suits by clients for breach of client confidentiality.

Banking and other financial supervisors worldwide have generally endorsed the Basel Principles which significantly covered all criminal proceeds and not only those resulting from drug trafficking. The compliance with these Principles represented a major self-regulatory initiative within the financial sector.

A further paper was issued by the Committee in October 2001 covering customer due diligence for banks. It addressed verification and Know Your Customer (KYC) standards with a cross-border aspect. This reflected the fact that earlier reviews of standards at a national level found large variations and frequent instances where standards could not be considered adequate. The setting of national standards was recognised to be the role of national supervisors but they were required to set these taking into consideration what other nations were being expected to do, to minimise variations in international standards.

The Basel Customer Due-Diligence Principles were drawn up for the banking sector; however, the FATF drew heavily on them when it undertook its 2003 revision of the Forty Recommendations (see Chapter 3).

OFFSHORE GROUP OF BANKING SUPERVISORS

The Offshore Group of Banking Supervisors (OGBS) was formed in Basel when representatives of a number of offshore centres met with members of the Basel Committee on Banking Supervision. The proposal to form an Offshore Group was welcomed by all concerned as a means of allowing offshore centres to define their common ground more clearly, to participate in the defining and implementation of international standards for cross-border banking supervision, and to hammer out a positive, constructive and coordinated response to the approaches made by other supervisory authorities for assistance in the effective supervision of international banks.

The conditions for membership of the OGBS include a requirement that a clear political commitment be made to implement the FATF's Forty Recommendations and the Nine Special Recommendations. Members of the OGBS who are not members of either the FATF or the CFATF (see Chapter 3) are formally committed to the Forty Recommendations through individual Ministerial letters sent to the FATF President during 1997–98. In 1999 they commenced mutual evaluations of those who were not FATF or CFATF members. However, these were subsequently replaced by the International Monetary Fund (IMF) assessments and the OGBS activity in developing the new methodology to be used for assessing compliance with the revised Forty Recommendations.

The countries listed below are all members of the Offshore Group of Banking Supervisors.

Aruba	Gibraltar	Mauritius
Bahamas	Guernsey	Netherland Antilles
Bahrain	Hong Kong, China	Panama
Barbados	Isle of Man	Singapore
Bermuda	Jersey	Vanuatu
Cayman Islands	Labuan	
Cyprus	Macau, China	

FINANCIAL STABILITY FORUM OFFSHORE FINANCIAL CENTRES (OFCs)

The Financial Stability Forum (FSF) was convened in April 1999 to bring together senior officials from 26 national authorities, six international financial institutions, seven international standard-setting, regulatory and supervisory groupings, two committees of central bank experts and the European Central Bank to promote international financial stability through information exchange and co-operation in financial supervision and surveillance.

In May 2000 the FSF encouraged a number of offshore centres to undertake necessary reforms and then requested the International Monetary Fund to put in place an assessment programme that would ensure long-term progress. As at the end of August 2004 almost all of the 42 countries which the FSF had identified as having offshore financial activities had undergone an initial assessment by the IMF.

The IMF assessments found that while shortcomings in the independence of the regulator, the level and quality of technical supervisory skills and onsite and offsite inspections were recurrent concerns, in general the wealthier OFC countries had a much higher rate of compliance with the standards than jurisdictions with a lower level of income. The lack by regulators and supervisors of adequate resources to undertake the work involved was also found to be a problem.

To enable individual OFCs to be evaluated by the world at large, the FSF strongly encouraged all countries to publish their IMF assessment reports. As at the end of August 2004 a total of 39 OFC countries had been assessed by the IMF, of which 24 had published their IMF assessment reports.

COMMONWEALTH SECRETARIAT

The Commonwealth Secretariat undertakes various activities in combating money laundering and terrorist financing throughout the Commonwealth. These include awareness raising and capacity building among member countries, particularly its developing members, provision of policy advice, identification and placement of experts and delivery of technical assistance to its member countries.

In May 1996 it produced a model law on the prohibition of money laundering. This provides a basis from which domestic legislation can be developed. In June of that year the Commonwealth Finance Ministers agreed to endorse a comprehensive and practical set of guidance notes for the financial sector, prepared by the Secretariat to help member countries introduce and implement effective anti-money laundering strategies.

These guidance notes were revised and updated in July 2000 and issued as a Code of Best Practice and were further revised in July 2003 to take account of the revised FATF recommendations and IMF methodology. Following the revision of the FATF's Forty Recommendations, the Commonwealth Secretariat in August 2004 further revised its Model of Best Practice for Combating Money Laundering and Terrorist Financing in the Financial Sector.

UNITED NATIONS

As noted earlier, the United Nations Convention Against Illicit Traffic in Narcotic Drugs and Psychotropic Substances, adopted in December 1988 in Vienna, was the first international measure to address the issue of proceeds of crime, and to require States to establish money laundering as a criminal offence. The Convention recognised that money generated by criminal activities is not difficult to hide and so proposed attacking trans-national criminals at their weakest point.

To ensure that there are no loopholes in the international machinery the UN Office on Drugs and Crime (UNODC) was mandated to assist States in the implementation and enactment of anti-money laundering legislation and internationally recognised standards in the regulation of financial services. Ten years later, in June 1998, at the UN General Assembly Special Session on drugs, a political declaration was adopted reaffirming the appropriateness of the strategy and the adoption of a plan of action 'Countering Money Laundering' to fine-tune and strengthen the action.

The UNODC has implemented a technical co-operation and research initiative known as the Global Programme against Money Laundering (GPML). The technical assistance provided by UNODC focuses on training in the field, such as sponsoring financial investigators and the development of practitioner tools. The GPML has also joined in a joint effort with the IMF and World Bank to form an expert working group to review and update the UNODC legislation on money laundering and the financing of terrorism.

The UN Security Council Resolutions of 1999 and 2001 (S/RES/1267 and S/RES/1373) requested each member within its jurisdiction to 'freeze the assets of terrorists and their associates, close their access to the international financial system and, consistent with its laws, make public the list of terrorists whose assets are subject to freezing'.

The Terrorism (United Measures) Order 2001 contains, *inter alia*, strict liability offences of making any funds or financially related services available to or for the benefit of terrorists.

INTERNATIONAL MONETARY FUND AND THE WORLD BANK

In November 2001 the IMF issued a communiqué calling on all members to ratify and fully implement the UN instruments to counter terrorism. These instruments were discussed above.

Then in the summer of 2002 the IMF and World Bank commenced a 12-month joint pilot programme of assessments of the international standards conducted with the FATF and OGBS. As previously mentioned, from the summer of 2002 to April 2004, 41 countries were assessed for compliance with the international standards.

The World Bank and the IMF during 2003–04 responded to requests from more than 100 countries to help them build institutional capacity to fight money laundering and terrorist financing. The technical assistance provided focused on how countries could bring their laws and regulatory systems up to international standards; improve coordination and co-operation between government departments and regional partners; as well as build institutional capacity for the financial sector.

In April 2004, the IMF and the World Bank agreed to adopt a more comprehensive and integrated approach to conducting assessments of compliance with international standards for preventing money laundering and countering terrorist financing, and to step up the delivery of technical assistance to those countries whose financial systems were most at risk. This approach recognised the revised FATF Forty Recommendations and the Nine Special Recommendations as the international standards for combating money laundering and terrorist financing. They have continued to work with the FATF, FATF-style regional bodies (FSRBs) and the OGBSs on the worldwide programme of anti-money laundering and counter-terrorist financing evaluations and assessments.

PARIS CONVENTION

Following the Conference of the European Parliament on 8 February 2002, a final declaration against money laundering was issued as an extension to the strategy contained in the second EU Directive. The proposals were set out under four separate headings:

- the transparency of capital movements;

- sanctions against unco-operative countries and territories;

- legal, police and administrative co-operation;

- prudential rules.

There are 30 proposals setting out the high-level objectives for development of the anti-money laundering regime in all EU member states, which also set out the future means for greater co-operation and information-sharing.

THE WOLFSBERG PRINCIPLES

In the late 1990s there was widespread international concern that private banks were not adequately involved in the fight against money laundering, particularly that involving corruption. To counter this concern an association known as the Wolfsberg Group consisting of ten, subsequently increased to 12, global banks working together with Transparency International was formed to produce and publish Anti-Money Laundering Principles for Private Banks. These Principles were first published in October 2000 and subsequently revised in May 2002.

To help counter the growing threat of terrorist financing, in January 2002 the Wolfsberg Group published a Statement on the Financing of Terrorism. This was enhanced in November 2002 by the publication of the Anti-Money Laundering Principles for Correspondent Banking.

The Group has continued its work and in September 2003 published a Statement on Monitoring, Screening and Searching.

While adoption of the Wolfsberg Principles is voluntary, there are strong commercial as well as regulatory reasons for all institutions undertaking private banking to adhere to the principles wherever possible as part of their risk management strategies.

EGMONT GROUP

The Egmont Group was founded at a meeting of the Financial Investigation Units (FIUs) of the various FATF countries held in Brussels in June 1995. The Group's aims are to increase and improve the communication between FIUs worldwide to help fight what is recognised as a universal problem. Well over 100 countries have so far created an FIU, the UK one being the National

Criminal Intelligence Service (NCIS) and, while not all are members of the Egmont Group, all are encouraged to join and as of June 2005 the Group had 101 members.

Following its creation, the Group established a Memorandum of Understanding under which intelligence can be shared between FIUs. Under this Memorandum the intelligence is owned by the FIU which is providing it and it can only be shared with another FIU if that FIU is independent from and not part of the investigation authorities.

At their creation in 1995 the Group defined an FIU as: 'A central national agency responsible for receiving, analysing and disseminating to the competent authorities disclosures of financial information concerning suspected proceeds of crime, or required by national legislation or regulation in order to combat money laundering.'

CHAPTER 3

Financial Action Task Force (FATF)

Following its creation in 1989 at the OECD economic summit in Paris, FATF has become the main international driving force in setting standards in the fight against money laundering and financing of terrorism. It is generally known for the issuing of its Forty Recommendations (see below), which now form the basis of most national laws on anti-money laundering. Its work continues and it has recently had its mandate extended until 2012. Its Presidency is a one-year position held by a senior government official appointed from among the FATF members. The President is supported by a small specialist Secretariat which is based in the Organisation for Economic Co-operation and Development (OECD) headquarters in Paris. However FATF, which was originally set up as an independent body, remains as such and is not part of the OECD.

Following the atrocities of 11 September 2001 in the USA, FATF issued an additional Nine Special Recommendations in respect of the prevention of terrorist financing.

MEMBERSHIP OF FATF

The minimum criteria for membership of FATF are as follows:

- To be fully committed at the political level to the prevention of money laundering.

- To implement the Recommendations within three years.

- To undertake annual self-assessment exercises and two rounds of mutual evaluations.

- To be a full and active member of the relevant FATF-style regional body, where such exists, or be prepared to work with the FATF or even to take the lead in establishing such a body.

- To be a strategically important country.

- To have already made the laundering of the proceeds of drug trafficking and other serious crimes a criminal offence.

- To have already made it mandatory for financial institutions to identify their customers and to report unusual or suspicious transactions.

For many years, the membership of FATF was restricted to the 26 principal industrialised countries. However, in 1998 it was recognised that in order to increase the effectiveness of the international anti-money laundering efforts there was a need to expand the membership to a limited number of strategically important countries which could play a major regional role. As a result, Argentina, Brazil and Mexico were admitted to membership in 2002 and South Africa and Russia in 2003. The membership of FATF as of February 2005 was made up of the following 31 member states and two regional bodies.

Argentina	Hong Kong	Russian Federation
Australia	Iceland	Singapore
Austria	Ireland	South Africa
Belgium	Italy	Spain
Brazil	Japan	Sweden
Canada	Luxembourg	Switzerland
Denmark	Mexico	Turkey
Finland	Netherlands	United Kingdom
France	New Zealand	United States of America
Germany	Norway	European Commission
Greece	Portugal	The Gulf Co-operation Council

China was granted Observer status in February 2005. The member states making up the Gulg Co-operation Council are shown below.

Bahrain	Qatar
Kuwait	Saudi Arabia
Oman	United Arab Emirates

In addition, the following FATF-style regional bodies hold Observer status.

- Asia/Pacific Group on Money Laundering (APG)

- Caribbean Financial Action Task Force (CFATF)

- Council of Europe Select Committee of Experts on the Evaluation of Anti-Money Laundering Measures (MONEYVAL) (formally PC-R-EV)

- Eurasian Group (EAG)

- Eastern and Southern Africa Anti-Money Laundering Group (ESAAMLG)

- Financial Action Task Force on Money Laundering in South America (GAFISUD)

- Middle East and North Africa Financial Action Task Force (MENAFATF).

These regional FATF-style bodies have similar form and functions to the FATF, and indeed some FATF members are also members of these regional bodies. These organisations are those which have, among other functions, a specific anti-money laundering mission or function.

In order to strengthen the worldwide fight against money laundering and terrorist financing, in June 2005 FATF held its first joint plenary meeting with one of its regional partners. This meeting took place in Singapore with APG. A total of 55 members were present at this joint meeting at which common interests were discussed. FATF proposes to continue to strengthen its relationships with regional partners by holding a joint typologies exercise with GAFISUD in November 2005 and a joint plenary meeting with ESAAMLG in February 2006.

It is considered that further major expansion of the membership is unlikely and, where it does occur, the potential new members are likely to be from areas where FATF is currently not significantly represented, in order to maintain a global balance. When China and India are admitted, it will bring the membership to 33 plus two regional bodies which, it is felt, will be the optimum number. FATF advise that any future identification of new members will address the issue of geographical balance and impact on the efficiency of FATF.

FATF also fulfils a number of other roles, including monitoring the progress of members in implementing anti-money laundering measures, analysing money laundering examples or case studies, and the worldwide promotion of anti-money laundering measures.

THE FATF FORTY RECOMMENDATIONS

FATF first published its Forty Recommendations aimed at governments and financial institutions in 1990. They form a comprehensive regime against money laundering and have been accepted worldwide as one of the most comprehensive bases for tackling money laundering. Indeed, since they were originally drawn up, more than 140 countries have signed up to them. Originally, they were restricted to drug trafficking as addressed by the Vienna Convention but, in 1996, FATF carried out a review which resulted in its Recommendations being extended to cover all crimes. The Recommendations, as amended in 2004, are shown in Appendix 5.

NON-CO-OPERATIVE COUNTRIES AND TERRITORIES (NCCT) LIST

In its report of February 2000 on this initiative FATF set out the 25 criteria for defining Non-Co-operative Countries and Territories (NCCTs). It also laid down the basic procedures for reviewing countries and territories. FATF established four regional review groups made up of representatives of FATF member governments. A total of 47 jurisdictions were chosen for review based upon the experiences of FATF members. The reviewers collated all the relevant laws, regulations and any other pertinent information and analysed these against the criteria. Reports were then written and discussed with the countries concerned. These reviews took place over two rounds during 2000 and 2001 and resulted in 23 jurisdictions being listed as NCCTs, 23 in 2000 and 8 in 2001.

So what are the consequences of being on the list? First, counter-measures can be applied to certain NCCTs that have not made adequate progress. The more important consequence which applies to all NCCTs is that Recommendation 21 should be imposed by all FATF members. This is important because if imposed it will have an effect on all their international dealings. This Recommendation states:

> *Recommendation 21*[1]
>
> *Financial institutions should give special attention to business relationships and transactions with persons, including companies and financial institutions, from countries which do not or insufficiently apply the FATF Recommendations. Whenever these transactions have no apparent economic or visible lawful purpose, their background and*

---

1   FATF Recommendation 21.

purpose should, as far as possible, be examined, the findings established in writing, and be available to help competent authorities. Where such a country continues not to apply or insufficiently applies the FATF Recommendations, countries should apply appropriate counter-measures.

This shows the importance from a country's point of view of being removed from and staying off the NCCT list.

Since the introduction of this list counter-measures have been imposed against some countries and the list, which has been subject to a number of reviews, has also been subject to a number of changes. These reviews and amendments continue and in the review of October 2005 the list was reduced to only the following two countries:

- Myanmar

- Nigeria.

These reviews will continue. While there are now only three countries on the list, it is conceivable that countries or territories could be added in future if they fail to continue to meet the FATF criteria. Indeed it is interesting that when you look at the NCCT criteria for assessing countries for inclusion on this list, one does have to question how many other jurisdictions might actually fail the test. At their meeting in Singapore in June 2005, FATF confirmed that the three remaining countries on the list had made progress towards embracing global anti-money laundering (AML) standards but they would continue to be monitored. However, FATF confirmed that the list would continue to exist and be used as necessary in the future. It also confirmed that those countries that had been recently de-listed would continue to be monitored for the issuance of secondary legislation and regulatory guidance.

FATF NINE SPECIAL RECOMMENDATIONS

As a result of the US terrorist atrocities on 11 September and the subsequent international actions and UN resolutions, FATF produced eight Special Recommendations on Terrorist Financing, which was subsequently increased to nine. The recommendations are shown in Table 3.1. Full details of the Special Recommendations can be found in Appendix 6.

Table 3.1   Financial Action Task Force Special Recommendations

I	Ratification and implementation of UN instruments
II	Criminalising the financing of terrorism and associated money laundering
III	Freezing and confiscating terrorist assets
IV	Reporting suspicious transactions related to terrorism
V	International co-operation
VI	Alternative remittance
VII	Wire transfers
VIII	Non-profit organisations
IX	Cash couriers

In October 2003, FATF issued a paper to supplement its Special Recommendations which set out International Best Practices for the Freezing of Terrorist Assets.[2] These best practices have been developed from the experiences of numerous countries around the world. They are designed to be best practice for the effective freezing of terrorist assets as well as in the development of national legal and procedural frameworks. What this paper clearly shows is that, in the fight against terrorism and its financing, there is a need for co-operation between the legal authorities and the private sector and indeed the public in general.

Many countries, however, have yet to fully implement these new recommendations. Whilst all are designed to prevent or curtail terrorist financing, the majority are equally applicable to all money laundering. Indeed, Special Recommendation IX specifically amends part of Recommendation 19.

TYPOLOGIES

Since its creation FATF, together with some of the regional bodies, has considered that one of the main purposes of its work is to undertake major studies into the methods and trends associated with money laundering and terrorist financing or, as they call them, typologies. It has thus worked over the years to identify money laundering trends and patterns. It has then, more importantly, considered new and emerging threats and attempted to come up with counter-measures. This information has then been made available not only to the appropriate authorities of each country but also the general public.

The typologies process is reviewed regularly and at the time of writing the most recent report was published in June 2005. It focused on a number of

---

2   Full details can be found at www.fatf-gafi.org.

different areas, one of which was 'money laundering and terrorist financing trends and indicators'. This latest topic is somewhat different from the others as it focuses on developing a 'methodology' to examine money laundering and terrorist financing. The project will obviously take some time and further reports will highlight progress and results.

The typologies exercises show areas of international concern. Help is given to frame countries' laws and regulations and to understand changes in money laundering patterns and techniques so that laws, regulations, operational investigations and reporting needs are kept fully up-to-date and relevant. The results of these exercises are available on the FATF website (www.fatf-gafi.org) and are an invaluable source of information and guidance to all those working in the anti-money laundering environment.

CHAPTER 4

European Directives

The European Union (EU) has issued two Directives on the Prevention of the Use of the Financial System for the Purpose of Money Laundering and at the time of writing is discussing a third. The Directives are designed to achieve a level playing field across the EU and their adoption is a condition of entry for all potential new members.

FIRST DIRECTIVE

In June 1991 the European Parliament and Council adopted the First European Directive on Prevention of the Use of the Financial System for the Purpose of Money Laundering. The Directive required all member states to amend their national laws so as to prevent their domestic financial systems from being exploited for the purposes of laundering money.

It was recognised in the Directive that the activity of money laundering can damage not only the individual institutions involved but the financial system as a whole and therefore the economy of an entire state and that of the EU. The Directive went on to recognise the vital role played by the financial institutions in the detecting and deterring of money laundering and required all financial institutions in member states to take certain measures to combat crime. This Directive became another important step in the international fight against money laundering and a way of preventing dirty money from being funnelled into the EU.

This first Directive was confined to credit and financial institutions as they were considered to be the most vulnerable to being used by money launderers, although member states were encouraged to extend the requirements to other industries/sectors where there was considered to be a risk of them handling money from criminals.

The Directive was also restricted to drug trafficking as defined in the Vienna Convention. However, member states were asked to consider extending it to other serious criminal activity. The extent to which any extension took place varied from member state to member state.

Member states were required to ensure, by implementing legislation as necessary, that:

- money laundering is prohibited;

- customer identification is verified and records kept;

- suspicious transactions are monitored and checked;

- institutions cooperate with the authorities by reporting suspicions and supplying relevant information;

- suspects are not 'tipped off' that they are being investigated;

- anyone reporting a suspicion is protected from actions from breach of confidence;

- institutions implement and maintain adequate internal controls and employee training.

SECOND DIRECTIVE

The limitations of the First Directive were the subject of extensive discussion throughout the Community and as a result extensive consultation took place on the introduction of a Second Directive. These consultations resulted in two major proposals. First, to extend the requirements from drug trafficking to encompass all serious crime including tax evasion together with an extension of the reporting requirements. The second, and more controversial, proposal was to bring within the terms of the Directive a number of non-financial-sector businesses.

These radical and extensive changes brought forth strong objections from various trade bodies, particularly those representing the legal and accountancy professions, at both a National and a Community level. Notwithstanding these objections, in December 2001 the European Parliament adopted the Second Directive to amend and extend the First. It also required that any future potential entrant country to the EU must adopt the Money Laundering Directives as a condition of entry.

The non-financial-sector businesses brought within the requirements were:

- auditors, external accountants and tax advisors;

- estate agents;

- notaries and other independent legal professions, when they participate in specified functions;

- dealers in high-value goods, such as precious stones or metals, or works of art;

- auctioneers, whenever payment is made in cash and for amounts of €15 000 or more;

- casinos.

The strategy of the Second Directive was further extended in 2002 by the final declaration of the Conference of European Parliaments. Details of the Paris Convention are fully discussed in Chapter 2.

The implementation of the Second Directive was effected in the UK by the Proceeds of Crime Act 2002 and the Money Laundering Regulations 2003. These will be fully discussed in Chapters 7 and 10 respectively when we will consider the practical effects of the Second Directive and the even more stringent and all-encompassing requirements enacted by the UK Government.

THIRD DIRECTIVE

When the Second Directive was adopted in 2001 it did not contain a precise definition of serious crime but left this to be reconsidered by the Commission, which was requested to present further proposals in 2004. Terrorist financing was also left to be dealt with under the heading of serious crime.

However, FATF subsequently made significant amendments to the 40 Recommendations which, it was considered, needed to be applied in a consistent manner across the EU. Consequently, it was agreed by the member states and the Commission that a completely new Directive to fully replace the First and Second Directives should be introduced.

This Directive was formally adopted in October 2005 and its final text appeared in the *European Journal* in November 2005. There is to be a two-year period for its adoption and hence should be implemented by all member states by the end of 2007. One of the main changes is contained in Article 7, which contains more detailed requirements for customer due diligence, but it is specified that those procedures should be conducted on a risk-sensitive basis. However, Article 11 specifies, as a minimum, three cases where the increased risk of money laundering necessitates enhanced due diligence:

- where there is no face-to-face contact with the customer;

- cross-frontier correspondent banking relationships; and

- relations with politically exposed persons (of which there is a new definition).

There have also been two important changes to the persons or firms covered by the Directive. The first is the addition of Trust and Company Service Providers who have now been brought fully within the terms of the Directive. Second, is a very important amendment to what has been known has 'high value dealers'. This section no longer specifies any particular industry or profession but now includes:

> *other natural or legal persons trading in goods, only to the extent that payments are made in cash in an amount of €15 000 or more, whether the transaction is carried out in a single operation or in several operations which appear to be linked.*[1]

As drafted this means that anyone who deals or sells in any goods for cash over €15 000 is now subject to the laws on anti-money laundering. This could in many countries expand very considerably the people having to comply with all the money laundering regulations and procedures.

There are a number of other important enhancements and changes the effects of which will only be fully apparent when the Directives requirements are actually implemented.

At the time of writing this book the UK Government have announced that they will undertake a consultation on way forward to commence in early 2006. This will lead to the production of draft regulations by late 2006 with the final regulations being issued by mid-2007 to enable the UK to implement the Directive within the two-year implementation period.

---

1   European Union 3rd Money Laundering Directive.

CHAPTER 5

US Legislation

The USA, in common with many other countries, has had anti-money laundering legislation in place for a number of years. Indeed, the USA was the first country to designate money laundering as a criminal offence. This was done by the introduction in 1986 of the Money Laundering Control Act (MLCA).[1] One of the main intentions of this Act, detailed in Section 1956, was to prevent transactional offences and transportation offences. This section defined 'transactional offences' as the conducting or attempted conducting of financial transactions involving the proceeds of 'specified unlawful activity' with the intention of promoting the unlawful activity, or with the knowledge that the transaction was designed to conceal the proceeds of unlawful activity or to avoid a transaction reporting requirement. As regards 'transportation offences' it also prohibited the transportation, transmission or transference of a monetary instrument into or out of the USA with the intent to promote some 'specified unlawful activity', or with the knowledge that they are the proceeds of unlawful activity or that the transportation is designed to conceal the proceeds or avoid a reporting requirement. The 'specified unlawful activity' actually refers to over 200 different US crimes ranging from narcotics trafficking through various kinds of fraud and counterfeiting to kidnapping. It also includes certain international crimes involving narcotics, certain violent crimes and crimes against foreign financial institutions. Section 1957 of the Act also prohibits knowingly engaging in a monetary transaction involving criminally derived property with a value greater than US $10 000.

One of the major areas of potential conflict in the MLCA was whether laundering money through a foreign bank was an offence. This was not clarified until 2001 on the passing of the US Patriot Act (see below).

Over the years, additional laws and requirements were imposed on US financial institutions requiring them to introduce and extend due diligence procedures, record-keeping, reporting and so on. These extensions, reviews and consultations took place over a number of years right up to the terrorist attacks of 11 September 2001; these atrocities led directly to the passing of the US Patriot Act.

---

1   Money Laundering Control Act of 1986, Subtitle H of Title I of the Anti-Drug Abuse Act of 1986.

US PATRIOT ACT

In a matter of weeks following 11 September, virtually all the anti-money laundering proposals that had been argued over for many months, or even in some cases years, were passed as part of The Uniting and Strengthening America Act by Providing Appropriate Tools Required to Intercept and Obstruct Terrorism Act, otherwise known as the US Patriot Act. Although this is a US Act, it has many provisions which are extra-territorial in application and therefore will have an effect on any institution around the world which has dealings in the USA or with a US-based bank. This is an extremely wide-ranging Act and became effective on 26 October 2001. It contains provisions on money laundering and counterfeiting, investigations and information sharing, criminal laws, transporting hazardous materials, federal grants, victims, immigration, and US domestic security. It also extends the requirements of the MLCA by including bribery of a public official. It also expands the list of 'offences against a foreign nation' which can constitute 'specified unlawful activities'. It also clears up the confusion as to whether laundering money through a foreign bank is an offence. Section 318 makes it a crime to launder money through foreign banks by expanding the MLCA to include financial transactions conducted through foreign banks. It does this by expanding the definition of 'financial institution' to include 'any foreign bank', as defined in Section 1 of the International Banking Act of 1978. This, of course, means that it is now an offence under US law to launder money exclusively through a foreign bank.

The provisions specifically relating to money laundering include an expansion of the money laundering laws and place more procedural requirements on banks. They also create the new crime of bulk cash smuggling and increase the statute of limitations on prosecuting some terrorism crimes. The Act amends the requirements in respect of reporting suspicious activity, anti-money laundering programmes, penalties for violating certain provisions such as record-keeping requirements, maintenance of bank records, and disclosures from consumer reporting agencies for counter terrorism investigations.

The money laundering procedural provisions allow the Secretary to the Treasury to require US domestic financial institutions and agencies to take certain measures when reasonable grounds exist for concluding that a foreign jurisdiction, financial institution outside the USA, a type of account or class of international transaction are of primary money laundering concern. These measures can include record-keeping, reporting requirements, identifying certain information about owners or accounts, and placing conditions on opening certain types of accounts.

The Act also:

- requires US financial institutions to create enhanced procedures for certain types of accounts to detect money laundering;

- prohibits US banks from maintaining certain accounts for foreign 'shell' banks;[2]

- requires the Secretary to the Treasury to set minimum standards for financial institutions to identify customers' opening accounts, including reasonable procedures to verify customers' identity, maintain that information, and consult lists of known or suspected terrorists or organisations provided by the government;

- requires regulations to encourage co-operation among financial institutions, regulators and law enforcement agencies to deter money laundering, including sharing information about individuals, entities and organisations engaged in or reasonably suspected of engaging in terrorist acts or money laundering;

- requires the Secretary to the Treasury to adopt regulations requiring securities brokers and dealers to submit suspicious activity reports. He may also adopt similar regulations for futures commission merchants, commodity trading advisors and commodity pool operators;

- includes as money laundering offences certain computer fraud crimes, certain export control violations, certain customs and firearms offences, and foreign corruption offences;

- allows for the forfeiture of the proceeds of foreign crimes found within the USA;

- allows for forfeiture in currency reporting cases;

- creates the new offence of harbouring or concealing terrorists;

- contains many further provisions for the prevention, detection and suppression of terrorism and terrorist activity;

---

2 'Shell' banks are defined as banks with no physical presence in any country and no appropriate affiliation with a regulated non-'shell' bank.

One of the most contentious parts of this Act is Section 317. This section gives the US Federal Courts jurisdiction over any foreign bank that maintains a bank account at a US financial institution for the purposes of adjudicating an action filed or enforcing a penalty ordered under the MLCA. This effectively means that if a foreign financial institution engages in a financial transaction which is proscribed in the MLCA then this institution may become subject to the jurisdiction of the US Federal District Courts, even if the transaction was carried out entirely outside the USA, simply because the foreign institution holds a bank account at a US financial institution.

Linked to the above is perhaps the most significant part of the Act in respect of money laundering and this revolves around 'Interbank' or 'correspondent' bank accounts. These two types of account are defined under US law as follows:

- An 'Interbank' account is defined under the US forfeiture laws as an account held by one financial institution for another financial institution primarily for the purpose of facilitating customer transactions.

- The US Patriot Act defines a 'correspondent' account as an account established to receive deposits from or make payments on behalf of a foreign financial institution, or handle other financial transactions related to such institutions. Such an account would include an 'Interbank' account.

The US authorities can now use such accounts as a gateway through which they can attempt to enforce US anti-money laundering laws extra-territorially.

One of the most contentious provisions is the power given to US Courts to seize funds held in a correspondent bank account held by a US financial institution for a foreign financial institution if those funds are the proceeds of unlawful activity. The Act decrees that funds deposited abroad shall be deemed to have been deposited into the Interbank or correspondent account in the USA. Consequently any restraining order, seizure warrant or arrest warrant in respect of such funds may be served on the US financial institution holding the account, and funds in the account up to the value of the funds deposited may be restrained, seized or arrested. Such funds can be forfeited to the US authorities if it can be established that the foreign bank received the proceeds of unlawful activity in an account at the foreign institution.

Such a forfeiture order can only be contested by the person or entity who is the owner of the funds. The owner is defined as the person or entity who was the owner of the funds when they were deposited into the foreign bank. The owner is not the foreign bank nor any intermediary institution involved in handling or transmitting the funds. The foreign institution from which the funds have been seized cannot therefore contest the forfeiture unless the forfeiture is the result of wrongdoing by the foreign bank. The US Government does not have to show a direct relationship between the funds forfeited and the criminally derived assets. This could leave the foreign financial institution in a very vulnerable situation and susceptible to double liability. This is because the Act may allow the US authorities to seize funds from an Interbank or correspondent account without relieving the foreign financial institution of its obligation to its clients and so, in some countries, the foreign institution may find itself civilly liable to the foreign depositor.

A foreign financial institution which, so far as its own country's law is concerned, has acted perfectly correctly could effectively face double jeopardy. This clearly cannot be right and could leave the institution in an impossible situation. However, at the time of publication the US Government had already begun to exercise the power which the Act gives it.

In addition to the forfeiture powers, this section of the Act also covers various aspects of record-keeping. The US financial institution must maintain additional records for any correspondent bank account it holds for a foreign financial institution. These records, which must be capable of being provided to the US authorities within seven days, must include details of the owner(s) of the foreign financial institution and the name and address of a US resident authorised by the foreign financial institution to accept service of legal process for records regarding the correspondent account. Also under this section the Secretary of the Treasury or the Attorney-General may issue a summons or subpoena to any foreign financial institution that maintains a correspondent account in the USA, and request records relating to such correspondent account, including records maintained outside the USA relating to the deposit of funds into the foreign institution. Should the foreign financial institution fail to comply with the summons or subpoena or fail to challenge it in the US Courts, the Secretary of the Treasury or the Attorney-General can issue a written notice to the US financial institution compelling it to terminate the correspondent banking relationship within ten working days.

The Act contains many more provisions and enforces more demands on US financial institutions and, directly or indirectly, on foreign financial institutions if they wish to do business in or through the USA, despite the requirements of their local law. The Act has fuelled a huge investment in staff, technology, record-keeping, monitoring and consultants. It is estimated that the financial services industry will have spent a total of US$10.9 billion on these initiatives by the end of 2005.

This section of the Act is clearly an effort by the US Government to put pressure on foreign financial institutions seeking access to the US financial system and markets, to enhance their anti-money laundering policies and procedures to reduce the risk that they will have funds seized from their accounts with a US institution.

Any person or institution undertaking business in the USA or with a US institution must be fully conversant with this Act and its implications. Many countries criticise the extra-territorial application of this Act but whether it is liked or not the fact remains that this Act and its requirements exist and are being enforced by the US Courts. The law is not static but is still being amended by further regulations issued by the Treasury department. It may not be comfortable or palatable, but the direction is clearly for more and not less extra-territorial reach. Non-US financial institutions and their clients must continue to monitor the situation in the USA if they are to avoid finding themselves in potentially serious legal difficulties.

CHAPTER 6

UK Legislation

The United Kingdom has been at the forefront of the international fight against money laundering. London, as one of the world's major financial centres, was seen as being particularly vulnerable to being used for money laundering. The UK, therefore, played a significant part in the setting up of FATF and in 1986 introduced its first anti-money laundering legislation. This was the Drug Trafficking Offences Act 1986. The next section details the development of legislation over time.

THE DEVELOPMENT OF LEGISLATION

While the Drug Trafficking Offences Act 1986 was restricted to drug trafficking-related money laundering, it was the first time that financial institutions had been required to report knowledge or suspicion of drug trafficking. At first sight this seemed sensible and simple. However, from a practical point of view it was not so easy. A financial institution might be genuinely suspicious of a customer or a particular transaction but might not have enough knowledge or information to decide whether the funds they were concerned about came from drug trafficking or some other criminal activity, including terrorism. In practice, they clearly could not know what the predicated offence was or indeed if there was one. This fact was recognised in the legislation and resulted at a very early stage in financial institutions reporting suspicions of funds, transactions or activities which arose from areas other than drug trafficking. In 1988 they were given, through the Criminal Justice Act, the same protection from civil suit for non-drug disclosures as for drug-related ones.

Over the following years the legislation in the UK, together with the Money Laundering Regulations 1993 used to implement the First EU Directive, extended the requirements to cover more and more offences. The result was a patchwork of legislation which was not always consistent and led to confusion in the minds of many people as to who were covered and who were not.

With the dawn of the new millennium, major changes and consolidation took place. This started in 2000 with increasing concern around the world about the funding of terrorism. The UK tidied up and consolidated its laws relating to this subject with the passing of the Terrorism Act 2000. This not only dealt with terrorist finances but laid out the pattern for the direction of future legislation on money laundering. The same year saw the passing of the Financial Services and Markets Act which, among other things, introduced and set up the Financial Services Authority (FSA). This was another major step in the fight against money laundering. The FSA was given four regulatory objectives, one of which was the reduction of financial crime. In Section 2 of the Act this is described as 'reducing the extent to which it is possible for a business carried on by a regulated person to be used for a purpose connected with financial crime'.[1] The FSA, when considering that objective, 'must have regard to the desirability of regulated persons taking adequate measures to prevent money laundering, facilitate its detection and monitor its incidence'.[2]

These extensive powers resulted in the FSA making several rules on the prevention of money laundering. These rules are enforced against all who have a licence from the FSA. While the vast majority are firms, there are some sole traders who are licensed in their own name – that is, a person – and this is achieved by the issue of its Money Laundering Sourcebook.[3] However, what many people do not realise is that the FSA's powers do not only apply to persons or firms it regulates. The Act gives the FSA the power to bring criminal prosecutions for breaches of Regulation 3 of the Money Laundering Regulations 2003 against any person or firm that is covered by the Regulations, regardless of whether that person or firm is regulated by the FSA. This prosecution power is over and above the severe regulatory action that the FSA can take against regulated persons or firms who fail to have appropriate systems and controls in place to prevent money laundering.

The terrorist attacks in the USA on 11 September 2001 prompted in the UK the passing of the Anti-terrorism, Crime and Security Act 2001. This Act not only gave the authorities greater powers but amended the money-laundering provision of the Terrorism Act in respect of terrorist financing, in particular the introduction of the 'objective test' which we will discuss in detail in Chapters 7 and 14. The amendments brought in by this Act also ensured that the Terrorism Act would reflect the appropriate requirements that had been agreed in the Second EU Directive and would bring it into line with what was being proposed in the then Proceeds of Crime Bill. This Act, however, also contains matters unrelated to terrorism and perhaps one of the most important from the UK's point of view, money laundering and crime in general, is Part 12. This Part deals with bribery and corruption and in particular the bribery of a foreign

---

1   Financial Services and Markets Act 2000.
2   Financial Services and Markets Act 2000.
3   Financial Services Authority Money Laundering Sourcebook.

officer or commission of bribery or corruption outside the UK. These sections make it a criminal offence in the UK to commit an act of bribery or corruption outside the UK (more on this in Chapter 8). This becomes important when we consider the implication of the Proceeds of Crime Act and in particular the reporting requirements. This will be discussed further in Chapter 8.

The next major and the most significant change and enhancement was the Proceeds of Crime Act 2002. This is one of the most wide-ranging pieces of legislation seen in modern times. This Act effectively repeals all previous anti-money laundering legislation and consolidates it into Part 7 of this Act. The only exception is the money laundering provisions which relate to the financing of terrorism. These remain part of the Terrorism Act 2000 as amended by the Anti-terrorism, Crime and Security Act 2001. It was not just a matter of consolidation but also an expansion to make it truly 'all crimes' legislation without a *de minimus* limit. The money laundering provisions of this Act and those of the Terrorism Act 2000 are, for practical purposes, identical and have also been drawn up so as to cover the appropriate requirements of the Second EU Directive. This Act was also subsequently amended, this time by the Serious Organised Crime and Police Act 2005. The practical implementation and difficulties of the Proceeds of Crime Act, even after its amendment, are fully discussed in Chapter 7.

The final piece of legislation in this series was made by way of a statutory instrument and is the Money Laundering Regulations 2003. These Regulations came into effect on 1 March 2004 to implement the Second EU Money Laundering Directive. They also replaced, consolidated and updated the Regulations of 1993 and 2001. These Regulations, like the Proceeds of Crime Act, have a number of practical difficulties and these are fully covered in Chapter 7.

To recap, UK law on the prevention of money laundering has now been consolidated into the following:

- Proceeds of Crime Act 2002 (as amended)

- Terrorism Act 2000 (as amended)

- Money Laundering Regulations 2003.

Although they seem straightforward, there are many practical problems which have not been fully considered or understood by those responsible for the implementation. Over the next few chapters we will consider in detail the requirements and offences detailed in these pieces of legislation. We will then go on to look at the implementation work necessary to meet and comply with these combined requirements. We will at the same time also consider the difficulties involved in complying with these requirements and the effect they have on businesses and their clients.

At the time of writing, the National Criminal Intelligence Service (NCIS) is the body to which all reports under either the Proceeds of Crime Act 2002 or the Terrorism Act 2000 are made. It is also the central point in respect of money laundering matters. Following the passing of the Serious Organised Crime and Police Act 2005, NCIS is to be absorbed into the Serious Organised Crime Agency in early 2006. For simplicity throughout this book this planned merger has been ignored and all references remain to NCIS except when reference is made to the Director-General of the Serious Organised Crime Agency as opposed to the Director-General of NCIS.

While meeting all the above requirements one must not lose sight of other legislation, in particular the Data Protection Act. This can pose a number of problems and potential conflicts with the anti-money laundering legislation. An example of a problem could be the information collected to meet the KYC (know your customer; see Chapter 12) requirements. This information is collected and stored under legal/regulatory requirements and falls within the exemption of the prevention and detection of crime. While this would cover the KYC information it does mean that such information collected to meet these requirements must only be held for that purpose and no other, without the customer's agreement. So the firm must ensure that its KYC information and records are not used, for example, for marketing. Another obvious danger is, if a customer makes a Subject Access Request under this Act, that you do not disclose a suspicion report you have made to NCIS or this could amount to 'tipping off'. Section 29 of the Act does allow for non-disclosure of such reports but it is not a blanket exemption and each case should be considered on its merits.

INDUSTRY GUIDANCE

From the very beginning the day-to-day interpretation of the law and regulations has been provided by guidance issued by industry bodies. This is recognised in Regulation 5 of the Money Laundering Regulations 1993 which provides that in determining whether a person or institution has complied with any of the requirements of the regulations, a court may take account of any relevant guidance issued or approved by a supervisory or regulatory body. In the absence of guidance issued by the regulators, relevant guidance may be provided by a trade association or other representative body.

From as early as 1990 the Financial Services Industry has followed the guidance notes produced by the Joint Money Laundering Steering Group (JMLSG). The membership of the JMLSG is currently made up of the following trade associations (see Table 6.1).

Table 6.1   Membership of the Joint Money Laundering Steering Group

Association of British Insurers	Council of Mortgage Lenders
Association of Foreign Banks	Electronic Money Association
Association of Friendly Societies	Finance and Leasing Association
Association of Independent Financial Advisors	Futures and Options Association
Association of Private Client Investment Managers and Stockbrokers	Investment Management Association
British Bankers Association	London Investment Banking Association
British Venture Capital Association	PEP & ISA Managers' Association
Building Societies Association	Wholesale Market Brokers' Association

The guidance notes have been amended and revised over the years as legislation and regulations have changed. Their aim is to outline the legislation and provide a practical interpretation of the Regulations and of the FSA Sourcebook requirements. They are also a source of good industry practice and provide management with advice and assistance.

Although the JMLSG guidance notes are intended for the UK financial sector they have been used by the trade bodies of other industries and professions either directly or to form the basis of their own guidance notes. They have also been used as a template in many other countries for advising their financial sectors.

CHAPTER 7

Proceeds of Crime Act 2002 – Part 7: Requirements and Offences

MONEY LAUNDERING REQUIREMENTS OF THE ACT

The money laundering provisions of this substantial and wide-ranging piece of legislation came into force on 24 February 2003. In this chapter we will look at the requirements of the Act so far as money laundering is concerned and the relevant money laundering offences. There are other parts of the Act that contain money laundering aspects, and these will be looked at in Chapter 8. The key effect of Part 7 of the Act is that the previous money laundering provisions, other than terrorism, have been consolidated and the predicate offences have been extended to all crimes, including petty theft as well as serious crime and tax evasion. There is no *de minimis* limit and it does not matter where the predicate offence took place so long as it would have been an offence if it had taken place in the UK. Some aspects of this Part of the Act have been amended by the Serious Organised Crime and Police Act 2005. These amendments have been made as appropriately to all the sections quoted below.

The purposes of this Act are:

- to create an Assets Recovery Agency;

- to consolidate, reform and update the criminal law in respect of money laundering;

- to make provision for the confiscation of the proceeds of crime;

- to allow for the recovery of any property which has been obtained through any unlawful conduct; and

- to provide for the search and seizure of cash which is reasonably suspected of having been obtained through unlawful conduct.

There are many practical operational difficulties with this legislation which, along with the Money Laundering Regulations 2003, forms the basis of UK anti-money laundering law. To understand them and to discuss the practical ways of meeting their requirements and the problems that may be encountered in doing so, it is necessary to examine the actual sections of the Act in detail to show what the law requires and just how all-encompassing its provisions are.

DEFINITIONS AND INTERPRETATIONS

However, before being able to consider the offences in detail there are three key definitions we need to fully understand as they affect all interpretations of the relative offences. These definitions are of criminal conduct, criminal property and money laundering. Section 340(2) states that:

> *Criminal conduct is conduct which:*
>
> a)   *constitutes an offence in any part of the United Kingdom, or*
>
> b)   *would constitute an offence in any part of the United Kingdom if it occurred there.*

At first sight this seems very broad but further examination shows the depth of the new law. Section 413(1) refers to 'any offence', which clearly includes summary offences. As a result, criminal conduct now includes minor criminal offences as well as serious ones. This gives rise to a number of potential dangers for while it is difficult to see how a summary-only offence might result in a money laundering transaction, the way the law is currently worded you could commit an offence if you handled money which should have been paid in respect of a parking fine. The absence of a *de minimis* limit also gives cause for concern, with many people considering it to be unintended or an oversight. However, this is not the case; the issues were debated at some length in Parliament and the government made it clear that it did not favour a *de minimis* provision.

The second definition, of criminal property, is defined in Section 340(3) as follows:

> *Property is criminal property if:*
>
> a)   *it constitutes a person's benefit from criminal conduct or it represents such a benefit (in whole or part and whether directly or indirectly), and*
>
> b)   *the alleged offender knows or suspects that it constitutes or represents such a benefit.*

As can be seen, there are two elements to the definition of criminal property: first, that the property is or represents a person's benefit from criminal conduct (as defined above) and, second, the alleged offender knows or suspects that this is the case. The understanding of this definition is vital if we are to fully understand the principal money laundering offences. This definition means that for the principal money laundering offences to be established, the alleged offender must know or suspect that the property is or represents the proceeds of crime. Property in this context is all property, whether situated in the UK or abroad, and includes money, property (real or personal and whether heritable or moveable), things in action, and other intangible property. It also includes an interest in land or a right in relation to property other than land.

These two important definitions must be read not only together but also with Sections 340(4) and 340(5). These state:

(4) It is immaterial

a)   *who carried out the conduct*

b)   *who benefited from it*

c)   *whether the conduct occurred before or after the passing of the Act*

(5) A person benefits from conduct if he obtains property as a result of or in connection with the conduct.

These definitions of criminal property and criminal conduct are important in our examination and consideration of the requirements of the Act but the third definition, that of money laundering, must also be fully understood before considering the principal offences.

Section 340(11) of the Act defines money laundering as follows:

Money laundering is an act which:

a)   *constitutes an offence under Sections 327, 328 or 329,*

b)   *constitutes an attempt, conspiracy or incitement to commit an offence specified in paragraph (a),*

c)   *constitutes aiding, abetting, counselling or procuring the commission of an offence specified in paragraph (a), or*

d)   *would constitute an offence specified in paragraph (a), (b) or (c) if done in the United Kingdom.*

So now we know what under UK law is meant by money laundering, criminal conduct and criminal property. The definitions are very wide and while the Act is designed to catch criminals, its implementation leads to a number of practical problems and difficulties, most of which we will discuss in this chapter. However, there are some problems which arise directly from the basic definitions which we have just considered, and we will look at these before proceeding to the statutory offences.

The definition of criminal property is directly linked to that of criminal conduct. It is with this last definition, of criminal conduct, that the problems arise. Under the definition, criminal conduct includes any activity abroad that would be an offence if it was carried out in the UK, regardless of whether it is an offence in the country where it is actually carried out. The problem from a practical point of view is determining when conduct outside the UK would constitute 'criminal conduct' for the purposes of the Act if committed in the UK. If the definition is taken literally one could have unintended situations developing – the one frequently used as an example is that of a UK citizen working in Spain as a bullfighter, which is perfectly legal conduct in Spain but criminal under UK law. Hence if the money derived from his occupation in Spain is brought into the UK, then an offence would have been committed. Thankfully this potential problem has been, at least partially, overcome by amendments made to Section 102 of the Serious Organised Crime and Police Act 2005. These create a defence to the principal money laundering offences under Sections 327 to 329 of the Proceeds of Crime Act and will be discussed later in this chapter. While much has been made of this problem and the action taken to resolve it one does have to question how often a 'bullfighter' requires financial services in the UK and how much of a problem it could be in reality.

Another problem is the scope of 'criminal conduct'. The question often raised is, do all criminal offences in the UK constitute 'criminal conduct' and do they, therefore, fall within the Act if they result in any form of benefit? It must be remembered that the Act has no *de minimis* provision and so catches all benefit or profit no matter how small and no matter how minor the crime.

Later in this chapter we will discuss the reporting requirements imposed by the Act on the 'regulated sector'. The confusion over what constitutes criminal conduct leads to uncertainty as to what is knowledge or suspicion of money laundering and hence needs to be reported. This confusion has led to numerous trivial and unnecessary reports being made to the authorities.

The new EU Third Directive should be able to clarify many of these points and establish a level playing field across the Community.

Let us now analyse the statutory offences and defences set out in Part 7. They fall into three categories:

- The three principal money laundering offences can be found in Sections 327, 328 and 329.

- Failure by a person in the regulated sector to report knowledge or suspicion of money laundering or where there are reasonable grounds for knowing or suspecting. This is contained in Sections 330 to 332.

- The offence of 'tipping off' contained in Sections 333 and 342.

Section 327: Concealing etc.[1]

(1) A person commits an offence if he:

(a)   *conceals criminal property;*

(b)   *disguises criminal property;*

(c)   *converts criminal property;*

(d)   *transfers criminal property; or*

(e)   *removes criminal property from England and Wales or from Scotland or from Northern Ireland.*

(2) But a person does not commit such an offence if:

(a)   *he makes an authorised disclosure under Section 338 and (if the disclosure is made before he does the act, mentioned in subsection (1)) he has the appropriate consent;*

(b)   *he intended to make such a disclosure but had a reasonable excuse for not doing so;*

(c)   *the act he does is done in carrying out a function he has relating to the enforcement of any provision of this Act or of any other enactment relating to criminal conduct or benefit from criminal conduct.*

(2A) Nor does a person commit an offence under subsection (1) if:

---

1   Proceeds of Crime Act 2002 – Section 327.

(a)   *he knows, or believes on reasonable grounds, that the relevant criminal conduct occurred in a particular country or territory outside the United Kingdom, and*

(b)   *the relevant criminal conduct:*

     (i)   *was not, at the time it occurred, unlawful under the criminal law then applying in that country or territory, and*

     (ii)   *is not of a description prescribed by an order made by the Secretary of State.*

(2B) In subsection (2A) 'the relevant criminal conduct' is the criminal conduct by reference to which the property concerned is criminal property

(2C) A deposit-taking body that does an act mentioned in paragraph (c) or (d) of Subsection (1) does not commit an offence under that subsection if:

(a)   *it does the act in operating an account maintained with it, and*

(b)   *the value of the criminal property concerned is less than the threshold (b) amount determined under Section 339A for the act.*

(3) Concealing or disguising criminal property includes concealing or disguising its nature, source, location, disposition, movement or ownership or any rights with respect to it.

Section 328: Arrangements[2]

(1) A person commits an offence if he enters into or becomes concerned in an arrangement which he knows or suspects facilitates (by whatever means) the acquisition, retention, use or control of criminal property by or on behalf of another person.

(2) But a person does not commit such an offence if:

(a)   *he makes an authorised disclosure under Section 338 and (if the disclosure is made before he does the act, mentioned in subsection (1)) he has the appropriate consent;*

---

2   Proceeds of Crime Act 2002 – Section 328.

(b)   he intended to make such a disclosure but had a reasonable excuse for not doing so;

(c)   the act he does is done in carrying out a function he has relating to the enforcement of any provision of this Act or of any other enactment relating to criminal conduct or benefit from criminal conduct.

(3) Nor does a person commit an offence under subsection (1) if:

(a)   he knows, or believes on reasonable grounds, that the relevant criminal conduct occurred in a particular country or territory outside the United Kingdom, and

(b)   the relevant criminal conduct:

(ii)   was not, at the time it occurred, unlawful under the criminal law then applying in that country or territory, and

(ii)   is not of a description prescribed by an order made by the Secretary of State.

(4) In subsection (2A) 'the relevant criminal conduct' is the criminal conduct by reference to which the property concerned is criminal property

(5) A deposit-taking body that does an act mentioned in Subsection (1) does not commit an offence under that subsection if:

(a)   it does the act in operating an account maintained with it, and

(b)   the arrangement facilitates the acquisition, retention, use or control of criminal property of a value that is less than the threshold amount determined under Section 339A for the act.

Section 329: Acquisition, use and possession[3]

(1) A person commits an offence if he:

(a)   Acquires criminal property;

(b)   Uses criminal property;

(c)   Has possession of criminal property.

---

3   Proceeds of Crime Act 2002 – Section 329.

(2) But a person does not commit such an offence if:

(a) *he makes an authorised disclosure under Section 338 and (if the disclosure is made before he does the act, mentioned in subsection (1)) he has the appropriate consent;*

(b) *he intended to make such a disclosure but had a reasonable excuse for not doing so;*

(c) *he acquired or used or had possession of the property for adequate consideration;*

(2A) Nor does a person commit an offence under subsection (1) if:

(a) *he knows, or believes on reasonable grounds, that the relevant criminal conduct occurred in a particular country or territory outside the United Kingdom, and*

(b) *the relevant criminal conduct:*

(i) *was not, at the time it occurred, unlawful under the criminal law then applying in that country or territory, and*

(ii) *is not of a description prescribed by an order made by the Secretary of State.*

(2B) In subsection (2A) 'the relevant criminal conduct' is the criminal conduct by reference to which the property concerned is criminal property

(2C) A deposit-taking body that does an act mentioned in paragraph (c) or (d) of Subsection (1) does not commit an offence under that subsection if:

(a) *it does the act in operating an account maintained with it, and*

(b) *the value of the criminal property concerned is less than the threshold amount determined under Section 339A for the act.*

(3) For the purposes of this section:

(a) *a person acquires property for inadequate consideration if the value of the consideration is significantly less than the value of the property;*

(b)   *a person uses or has possession of property for inadequate consideration if the value of the consideration is significantly less than the value of the use or possession;*

(c)   *the provision by a person of goods or services which he knows or suspects may help another to carry out criminal conduct is not consideration [sic].*

DEFENCES

So despite these amendments we can see how wide and all-encompassing these principal offences are. So what are the defences to these sections? First, we have to remember that for certain requirements of the Act there are two different classes of people – those within the regulated sector and those outside it, whom I will refer to as the 'ordinary public'. Those in the 'regulated sector' have special, more demanding, requirements which we will discuss later. So let us look first at the ordinary public.

The first important thing to always remember that to commit any offence under these sections you must be dealing with 'criminal property'. This is why when we discussed it earlier the definition of 'criminal property' was considered so important. In most day-to-day dealings the ordinary public are genuinely unlikely to know or suspect that they could be handling the benefits of criminal conduct, unless they themselves committed the underlying crime, and therefore they would not be committing an offence under Sections 327, 328 or 329. However, let us look at a situation where someone does know or suspect that the property they are handling or proposing to handle is the proceeds of criminal conduct: what then? Well, under all three sections a person does not commit an offence if they make an authorised disclosure and if the disclosure is made before they carry out the prohibited act, and they have the appropriate consent. Alternatively, there is provision for an authorised disclosure to be made after the alleged offender does the prohibited act, if there is good reason for the failure to disclose before they did the prohibited act and the disclosure is made under their own initiative and as soon as is practicable for them to make it.

The other defences are that a person intended to make a disclosure but had a reasonable excuse for not doing so, or the act is done in the carrying out of a function relating to the enforcement of any provision of the Act or of any other enactment relating to criminal conduct or benefit from criminal conduct. Such a situation would arise where the police or other authority took possession of criminal property in the course of their official duties. If this property was cash and the police deposited it at a bank for safe-keeping then the bank holding the account would claim the same defence. The problem with the first of these defences, that of reasonable excuse, has an additional problem since the Act gives no definitions of 'good reason' or 'reasonable excuse' nor is there currently any judicial interpretation. That makes the use of this defence extremely risky and only time will tell to what practical use it can be put.

There remains one final defence, that of adequate consideration, which applies to Section 329 only. This defence is so that people, such as tradespeople, who are paid for ordinary consumable goods and services in money that comes from crime, are not under any obligation to question the source of the money. This defence may also apply to the services provided by professional advisors such as accountants and solicitors. However, the fees charged or to be charged would have to be reasonable in respect of the work carried out or to be carried out. However, the section also makes it absolutely clear that the provision by a person of goods or services which they know or suspect may help another person to carry out criminal conduct is not adequate consideration and hence the defence will not be available.

All the above offences carry a maximum penalty of 14 years' imprisonment and/or a fine and liability to a confiscation or civil recovery order.

As already mentioned, the Serious Organised Crime and Police Act 2005 has also added an additional defence to each of the above three sections. It is the same wording for each section and is:

Nor does a person commit an offence under subsection (1) if:

    (a)   *he knows, or believes on reasonable grounds, that the relevant criminal conduct occurred in a particular country or territory outside the United Kingdom, and*

    (b)   *the relevant criminal conduct:*

        (i)   *was not, at the time it occurred, unlawful under the criminal law then applying in that country or territory, and*

        (ii)   *is not of a description prescribed by an order made by the Secretary of State.*

So while this amendment has overcome one practical issue it may lead to another since, as at the time of writing this book, we do not know what 'orders' the Secretary of State is going to issue. Another potentially difficult amendment made by the Serious Organised Crime and Police Act is the addition of a new condition for reporting; that of:

> *that he believes, or it is reasonable to expect him to believe, that the information or other matter mentioned in subsection (3) will or may assist in identifying that other person or the whereabouts of any of the laundered property.*[4]

The potential problem with this new requirement is how is an employee in, say, a bank going to know or reasonably believe that they have such information? Will they be able to understand what information may be of use? The aim of the Act is quite clear but, as you can see, there are likely to be a few practical problems in properly implementing it. If people are uncertain then it will either lead to failure to report or, more likely, many unnecessary reports being made 'just in case' or to be 'on the safe side'.

'REGULATED SECTOR' OFFENCES

While the above offences can be committed by anyone there are some that are restricted to those in the 'regulated sector'. These constitute the second category of offences and are contained in Sections 330 to 332. These offences are punishable on conviction by a maximum of five years' imprisonment and/or a fine. The requirements of these sections are what most people think about when they talk about money laundering. They are the ones which result in the most involvement between the 'public' and the 'authorities' and are those that give the greatest potential for problems and difficulties. Before considering these sections, it is necessary to fully understand what is meant by the 'regulated sector'. The Act clearly defines what is meant by the regulated sector and it means what one would assume it to mean: banks, insurance companies and other financial institutions. However, following the issuance of the Money Laundering Regulations 2003 it was necessary for this definition to be substantially amended to bring it into line with the industries covered by the Regulations. Accordingly another statutory instrument known as the Proceeds of Crime Act 2002 (Business in the Regulated Sector and Supervisory Authorities) Order 2003 was made. This expanded the definition to ensure that all the parties covered by the Second EU Directive and hence the Money Laundering Regulations 2003 fell within the definition of the 'regulated sector'. So the definition now covers not only all financial institutions including bureaux

---

4   Serious Organised Crime and Police Act 2005 – Section 104.

de change and money transmitters but also those engaged in estate agency work, operating casinos, insolvency practitioners, tax advisors, provision of accountancy services and audit services, the provision of legal services which involve participation in financial or property transactions, business services in relation to the formation, operation or management of a company or trust, and dealers in goods where any single transaction or series of linked transactions involves accepting cash in excess of €15 000. The requirements for these additional industries and professions are considered in greater detail under the Money Laundering Regulations 2003. Having looked at the definition, let us now look at the requirements in detail.

Section 330: Failure to disclose: regulated sector[5]

(1) A person commits an offence if the conditions in subsections (2) to (4) are satisfied.

(2) The first condition is that he:

    (a)   knows or suspects, or

    (b)   has reasonable grounds for knowing or suspecting, that another person is engaged in money laundering.

(3) The second condition is that the information or other matter:

    (a)   on which his knowledge or suspicion is based, or

    (b)   which gives reasonable grounds for such knowledge or suspicion, came to him in the course of a business in the regulated sector.

(3A) The third condition is:

    (a)   that he can identify the other person mentioned in subsection (2) or the whereabouts of any of the laundered property, or

    (b)   that he believes, or it is reasonable to expect him to believe, that the information or other matter mentioned in subsection (3) will or may assist in identifying that other person or the whereabouts of any of the laundered property.

(4) The fourth condition is that he does not make the required disclosure to:

    (a)   a nominated officer, or

---

5   Proceeds of Crime Act 2002 – Section 330.

(b)   a person authorised for the purpose of this Part by the Director
         General of the Serious Organised Crime Agency as soon as is
         practicable after the information or other matter mentioned in
         subsection (3) comes to him.

(5) The required disclosure is a disclosure of:

(a)   the identity of the other person mentioned in subsection (2),
         if he knows it,

(b)   the whereabouts of the laundered property, so far as he knows
         it, and

(c)   the information or other matter mentioned in subsection (3).

(5A) The laundered property is the property forming the subject matter
of the money laundering that he knows or suspects, or has reasonable
grounds for knowing or suspecting, that other person to be engaged in.

(6) But a person does not commit an offence under this section if:

(a)   he has a reasonable excuse for not making the required
         disclosure,

(b)   he is a professional legal adviser and:

   (i)   if he knows either of the things mentioned in subsection
            (5)(a) and (b), he knows the thing because of information or
            other matter that came to him in privileged circumstances,
            or

   (ii)   the information of other matter mentioned in subsection
            (3) came to him in privileged circumstances, or

(c)   subsection (7) applies to him.

(7) This subsection applies to a person if:

(a)   he does not know or suspect that another person is engaged in
         money laundering, and

(b)   he has not been provided by his employer with such training as
         is specified by the Secretary of State by order for the purposes
         of this section.

(7A) Nor does a person commit an offence under subsection (1) if:

(a)   he knows, or believes on reasonable grounds, that the money laundering is occurring in a particular country or territory outside the United Kingdom, and

(b)   the money laundering:

    (i)   is not, unlawful under the criminal law then applying in that country or territory, and

    (ii)   is not of a description prescribed by an order made by the Secretary of State.

(8) In deciding whether a person committed an offence under this section the court must consider whether he followed any relevant guidance which was at the time considered:

(a)   issued by a supervisory authority or any other appropriate body,

(b)   approved by the Treasury, and

(c)   published in a manner it approved as appropriate in its opinion to bring the guidance to the attention of persons likely to be affected by it.

(9) A disclosure to a nominated officer is a disclosure which:

(a)   is made to a person nominated by the alleged offender's employer to receive disclosures under this section, and

(b)   is made in the course of the alleged offender's employment and in accordance with the procedure established by the employer for the purpose.

(10) Information or other matter comes to a professional legal adviser in privileged circumstances if it is communicated or given to him:

(a)   by (or by a representative of) a client of his in connection with the giving by the adviser of legal advice to the client,

(b)   by (or by a representative of) a person seeking legal advice from the adviser, or

(c)   by a person in connection with legal proceedings or contemplated legal proceedings.

(11) But subsection (10) does not apply to information or other matter which is communicated or given with the intention of furthering a criminal purpose.

(12) Schedule 9 has effect for the purpose of determining what is:

(a)   *a business in the regulated sector;*

(b)   *a supervisory authority.*

(13) An appropriate body is any body which regulates or is representative of any trade, profession, business or employment carried on by the alleged offender.

This is a long and very complex section but a vital one for any person or organisation falling within the regulated sector. This is the section which from a day-to-day point of view is perhaps one of the most important for those within the regulated sector, but must be considered in conjunction with Sections 327 to 329.

So what does all this actually mean? Put simply, if anyone in the regulated sector knows or suspects, or there are reasonable grounds for knowing or suspecting from information or other sources which has come to them in the course of their business, that another person is engaged in money laundering then they must make a report. This reporting requirement is regardless of the amounts involved or the nature of the underlying crime that produced the assets to be laundered. The obligation to report also covers attempted money laundering regardless of whether the business has been undertaken or turned down. They must report this as soon as is reasonably practicable as directed by the Director-General of the National Criminal Intelligence Service (NCIS) and in the form and manner prescribed by him. Simply telephoning the local police station or speaking to a passing police officer is not an authorised disclosure and would not meet the requirements of the Act. If the knowledge or suspicion arises before the transaction is undertaken then when making the report the consent of the NCIS must be sought to carry out the transaction. We will discuss the problems involving consent later in this chapter. This all sounds straightforward, but is it in practice?

KNOWLEDGE

Let's break this down further. To start with, what do we mean by 'knowledge'? 'Knowledge' means actual knowledge. Any extension of this to subjective knowledge or constructive knowledge – for example, wilful blindness – has yet to be determined in a prosecution for an offence of money laundering. To have actual knowledge of money laundering will in practice be a very rare occurrence. It would also be difficult for the prosecution to prove that someone had actual knowledge of money laundering and had failed to report it.

SUSPICION

So what about suspicion? Suspicion is subjective and personal. It falls well short of proof based on firm evidence. Suspicion has been defined by the courts as being beyond mere speculation and being based on some foundation. It has therefore been described as having to have a degree of satisfaction not necessarily amounting to belief but at least extending beyond speculation as to whether or not an event has occurred. Also, although the creation of suspicion requires a lesser factual basis than the creation of a belief, it must nonetheless be built upon some foundation.

Here again it is difficult to prove in a court that someone was suspicious and, having had that suspicion, failed to report it. This is believed by many to be one of the reasons why, under the old law, some people did not report, knowing it was virtually impossible to prosecute them and so turned a blind eye to the situation. Under the Proceeds of Crime Act, however, the situation has changed at least so far as the regulated sector is concerned. As is shown above under Section 330, a report does not have to be made purely where there is knowledge or suspicion but also where there are 'reasonable grounds for knowing or suspecting'. This effectively changes it from a subjective test to an objective one. This means that to show that an offence of no reporting has taken place it is no longer necessary to prove that someone knew or suspected; all that is necessary is to be able to show there were reasonable grounds on which an honest and reasonable person would have known or suspected.

So what are reasonable grounds? This is a very good question and it is something which is not fully defined or fixed in English law. However, the objective test must clearly arise when there are proved to be facts or circumstances from which an honest and reasonable person engaged in a business in the regulated sector would have inferred knowledge or formed the suspicion that another person was engaged in money laundering. This 'objective test' or 'reasonable grounds test' is also known as the 'negligence test'. This expansion of the reporting requirements means that anyone in the regulated sector can commit the offence not because they actually knew or suspected but because there were grounds on which a reasonable professional should have known or suspected.

So now we have it. If you are in the 'regulated sector' and you know or suspect or there are reasonable grounds for knowing or suspecting that someone is engaged in money laundering then you must make a report unless you fall within one of the exclusions mentioned above. Failure to make the report is an offence itself and is over and above any other offences which may have taken place. There are one or two limited defences to failing to report, which are detailed above. So how, when and to whom would such reports be made? Within the regulated sector the disclosure is normally made to the officer nominated by the person's employer, who will make any suitable report to the NCIS. By making the disclosure this way the employee who has the knowledge or suspicion will satisfy their responsibilities. Section 331 sets out the responsibilities of this nominated officer as follows:

THRESHOLD

The Serious Organised Crime and Police Act 2005 has at Section 103 introduced an important defence known as 'the threshold' and which amends Sections 327 to 329 but which is restricted to deposit-taking bodies only. For this purpose a deposit-taking body is defined as 'a business which engages in the activity of accepting deposits or the National Savings Bank'. The concept is to relieve banks of the need to report and/or seek consent for each and every small cheque that is presented after a suspicion report has been filed. This is a practical solution to a time- and resource-consuming problem that achieved very little for all the work done. It should be easy to implement and apply although there is one small potential practical difficulty. So long as the threshold amount is the standard £250 quoted in the Act it should be easy to program systems to operate using this figure across the board. However, the Act does allow for a constable or an officer of Revenue and Customs to vary this amount. Not only can they vary the amount upwards for a particular account, they can also vary the amount both upwards and downwards for different 'acts' carried out on an account. Trying to implement such varying limits on an account-by-account or even transaction-by-transaction basis is bound to lead to problems and errors. Institutions·are going to have to be very careful about how they handle this, and indeed the resources needed to achieve it may end up being greater than those that would have been used to make reports for each transaction.

> *Section 331: Failure to disclose: nominated officers in the regulated sector*[6]
>
> *(1) A person nominated to receive disclosures under Section 330 commits an offence if the conditions in subsections (2) to (4) are satisfied.*

---

6   Proceeds of Crime Act 2002 – Section 331.

(2) The first condition is that he:

(a)   *knows or suspects, or*

(b)   *has reasonable grounds for knowing or suspecting, that another person is engaged in money laundering.*

(3) The second condition is that the information or other matter:

(a)   *on which his knowledge or suspicion is based, or*

(b)   *which gives reasonable grounds for such knowledge or suspicion came to him in consequence of a disclosure made under Section 330.*

(3A) The third condition is:

(a)   *that he knows the identity of the other person mentioned in subsection (2) or the whereabouts of any of the laundered property, in consequence of a disclosure made under Section 330,*

(b)   *that that other person, or the whereabouts of any of the laundered property, can be identified from information or other matter mentioned in subsection (3), or*

(c)   *that he believes, or it is reasonable to expect him to believe, that the information or other matter will or may assist in identifying that other person or the whereabouts of any of the laundered property.*

(4) The fourth condition is that he does not make the required disclosure to a person authorised for the purpose of this Part by the Director General of the Serious Organised Crime Agency as soon as is practicable after the information or other matter mentioned in subsection (3) comes to him.

(5) The required disclosure is a disclosure of:

(a)   *the identity of the other person mentioned in subsection (2), if he disclosed to him under Section 330,*

(b)   *the whereabouts of the laundered property, so far as disclosed to him under Section 330, and*

(c)   *the information or other matter mentioned in subsection (3).*

(5A) The laundered property is the property forming the subject-matter of the money laundering that he knows or suspects, or has reasonable grounds for knowing or suspecting, that other person to be engaged in.

(6) But he does not commit an offence under this section if he has a reasonable excuse for not making the required disclosure,

(6A) Nor does a person commit an offence under subsection (1) if:

(a)   *he knows, or believes on reasonable grounds, that the money laundering is occurring in a particular country or territory outside the United Kingdom, and*

(b)   *the money laundering is not unlawful under the criminal law then applying in that country or territory, and*

(c)   *is not of a description prescribed by an order made by the Secretary of State.*

(7) In deciding whether a person committed an offence under this section the court must consider whether he followed any relevant guidance which was at the time concerned:

(a)   *issued by a supervisory authority or any other appropriate body,*

(b)   *approved by the Treasury, and*

(c)   *published in a manner it approved as appropriate in its opinion to bring the guidance to the attention of persons likely to be affected by it.*

This is an important section for the entire anti-money laundering process throughout the regulated sector. This section was introduced at the Committee stage in the House of Lords. From the debates it appears that there was concern that nominated officers would not necessarily pass on reports to the NCIS and accordingly this section was introduced to provide greater clarity as to the role and responsibilities of the nominated officer. In fact the appointment of a nominated officer is not actually a requirement of the Act. However, under regulation 7 of the Money Laundering Regulations 2003, firms in the regulated sector must appoint a nominated officer. Thus, each firm in the regulated sector has such an officer and this position is a mainstay of the whole anti-money laundering process.

As already stated, employees will make reports to the nominated officer under Section 330 so as to avoid committing an offence. On receipt of such reports the nominated officer must consider them, based upon all the information available, and then decide whether he or she knows or suspects that another person is engaged in money laundering. There will be occasions when although an employee is suspicious, a nominated officer with the benefit of greater experience or greater access to business and customer information may decide that they do not have any knowledge or suspicion or any reasonable grounds for any knowledge or suspicion.

The Act goes on to say that a nominated officer will commit an offence if three conditions are satisfied:

- *he knows or suspects or has reasonable grounds for knowing or suspecting that another person is engaged in money laundering;*

- *he receives the information or other matter, on which his knowledge or suspicion is based or which gives reasonable grounds for such knowledge or suspicion, as a consequence of a disclosure made under Section 330;*

- *he does not make the required disclosure as soon as is practicable after the information came to him.*

In the event of any action being taken under the Proceeds of Crime Act against a nominated officer the Courts must take into account whether or not he or she has followed any relevant guidance issued by the Joint Money Laundering Steering Group or other similar body which has been approved by HM Treasury.

Section 331 of the Act also provides that a nominated officer does not commit an offence if he or she has a reasonable excuse for not disclosing the information or other matter. This seems acceptable at first sight but, unfortunately, there is no judicial guidance or advice on what might constitute a reasonable excuse. So were does this leave the nominated officer? As they stand, these provisions can leave the nominated officer feeling quite vulnerable. This is likely to make nominated officers, particularly less experienced ones, take a cautious approach and report in all cases in order to protect themselves. This over-cautious reporting is likely to cause problems for both the nominated officer and the institution. It can also result in delays in obtaining 'appropriate consent', with which there are already enough problems, as we will discuss shortly.

Disclosures must be made either electronically over the MoneyWeb system or by using the proscribed form which was amended by the Serious Organised Crime and Police Act. A sample of this proscribed report can be found on the

NCIS website (www.ncis.co.uk/disclosure). All such reports must be made to an NCIS officer. It is not sufficient for the nominated officer to disclose to a Customs officer or a constable as it would have been under previous legislation.

PRE-EVENT DISCLOSURES

The question of making a pre-event disclosure and obtaining 'consent' to proceed with the transaction is an area that frequently gives everyone involved great cause for concern and worry, often quite unnecessarily.

When a suspicion arises before the transaction or other event is due to take place, the nominated officer must make a report to the NCIS and seek their consent to undertake the transaction. Until that consent is obtained the transaction or other event cannot proceed. NCIS has a time limit of seven working days in which they must respond, otherwise the 'reporter' is entitled to assume that consent has been granted. The seven working days commences following receipt by the NCIS of the report. So that there is no confusion, working days are defined as a day other than a Saturday, Sunday, Christmas Day, Good Friday or a day which is a bank holiday under the Banking and Financial Dealings Act 1971 in the part of the UK in which the nominated officer is situated.

In practice the vast majority of consent requests are granted well within the seven working-day period. However, this can still result in problems and delays in completing a transaction because of the timing of the suspicion and hence the report. The sheer mechanics of dealing with such consent requests have their own time delay. So, for example, if the report is not made until, say, two days before completion date it will not be possible, in most cases, to get the consent back from the NCIS by the completion date and so the transaction will have to be delayed.

Of perhaps even greater difficulty for the nominated officer and his institution are those, thankfully few, cases when consent is refused. This means that the institution cannot undertake the transaction. This inability continues for a moratorium period of up to 31 days starting with the date that consent was refused. This moratorium period allows the authorities time to undertake further enquiries and investigations but it leaves the institution in an almost impossible position. It is now unable to carry out its client's instruction and so is vulnerable to action being against it for this 'failure'. However, it is unable to tell the client the reason for its failure since it is now aware that an investigation is being undertaken and so any communication of this to the client could amount to 'tipping off' (see later in this chapter) as it may prejudice that investigation. This problem is also compounded by the fact that although the NCIS can statutorily give or refuse consent, it does not undertake any enquiries or investigations. These are done by the investigating authorities, that is, the police or Customs and Excise. However, all communications with them in these circumstances must be through the NCIS which can add further delays and problems.

This is one of the potentially most problematical areas of the whole Act. The nominated officer will have to set up and manage a system to handle all consent reports. This system will have to be designed so as to prevent transactions being completed before consent is received. It must also ensure that no request is overlooked or forgotten and to chase if replies are not received. The seven-day rule must also be carefully monitored and, if necessary, activated should no response be forthcoming from the NCIS. Staff from financial institutions also have to manage dealings with clients when transactions are delayed because of waiting for consent. Perhaps, however, the most difficult cases to manage and handle will be those where consent has been refused. Throughout, staff must constantly be aware of the 'tipping off' provisions. This is an area that will require the utmost skill in its management and control, and we will discuss it further in Chapter 14.

'TIPPING OFF'

One of the most frequently heard topics of discussion when people are speaking of money laundering is 'tipping off'. It is an area that, while fraught with danger, is often misunderstood and frequently exaggerated. However, it is very important, as can be seen under 'consent'.

To understand it we need to look at both Sections 333 and 342 of the Act. This latter Section is not in Part 7 but is part of Part 8. However, it is so closely linked with Section 333 as they both relate to tipping off offences that they must be considered together.

Section 333 applies when a report has been made to the NCIS, and subsection 1 states:

> *A person commits an offence if:*
>
>   *(a)*   *he knows or suspects that a disclosure falling within Section 337 or 338 has been made, and*

(b)   *he makes a disclosure which is likely to prejudice any investigation which might be conducted following the disclosure referred to in paragraph (a).*

Section 342 applies if a person knows or suspects that an appropriate officer is acting (or proposing to act) in connection with a confiscation investigation, a civil recovery investigation or a money laundering investigation which is being or is about to be conducted. At subsection 2 it states:

(a)   *he makes a disclosure which is likely to prejudice the investigation, or*

(b)   *he falsifies, conceals, destroys or otherwise disposes of, or causes or permits the falsification, concealment, destruction or disposal of, documents which are relevant to the investigation.*

Both sections contain similar defences:

- he does not know or suspect that the disclosure was likely to be prejudicial or is likely to prejudice the investigation or that the documents are relevant to an investigation or that he does not intend to conceal any facts disclosed by the documents;

- the disclosure is made in the exercise of a function under this Act or any other enactment relating to criminal conduct or benefit from criminal conduct or in compliance with a requirement imposed under or by virtue of this Act; or

- he is a professional legal adviser and the disclosure is given by the adviser in connection with the giving of legal advice to the client or to any person in connection with legal proceedings or contemplated legal proceedings.

In general terms, someone could possibly commit the offence of 'tipping off' if they disclose information, to any person, that is likely to prejudice an existing or potential future investigation if they know or suspect that a suspicion report has been made to a nominated officer or to the NCIS. The offence can now take place as soon as an internal suspicious report has been made to the nominated officer. Reading the two sections together, the definition of a disclosure is unlimited and can, therefore, extend beyond intentional disclosure but also inadvertent disclosure. So clumsy handling of a client relationship following a disclosure or service of a court order could amount to tipping off. One must also not forget that under Section 342 the offence also includes the act of falsifying, concealing, destroying or otherwise disposing of documents. This is of particular concern following the service of a court order. However, it could also apply when, having made a disclosure, one then destroyed the documents and records on which the disclosure was based.

So while this is a complicated and, in some ways, dangerous section, with thorough understanding and careful management of all your information and records you should be able to assume that you should not fall foul of it.

Having considered Part 7 of the Proceeds of Crime Act 2002 in this chapter, in Chapter 8 let us turn to look at the other aspects of the Act that relate to money laundering.

Proceeds of Crime Act 2002 – Other Areas

In Chapter 7 we discussed Part 7 of the Proceeds of Crime Act 2002 which contains the money laundering offences and requirements. To many people, Part 7 is the only part of the Act that impacts upon the subject of money laundering and so is the only area they need to be concerned with. However, there are many other aspects of this Act which can have an effect on institutions or, indeed, the public at large.

There are three main aspects that need to be considered, the most important one being Part 8 which deals with the major investigations in respect of money laundering. However, perhaps the biggest change brought about by the Act is to be found in Part 1 which is the creation of the Assets Recovery Agency. Whilst this is a relatively small part of the Act the creation of this new Agency is a major innovation in UK laws. Both the implications and work of this new Agency also appear throughout all the other parts of the Act including Part 8.

PART 8 – INVESTIGATIONS

There are three types of investigations which can be undertaken under this Act. These are confiscation investigations, civil recovery investigations and money laundering investigations. Any of these investigations can involve an institution and their most likely involvement with this Part of the Act will revolve around one of the various orders which can be served upon the institution. One of the most important things to remember with these orders is that they are obtained *ex parte* – that is, the order is obtained without the knowledge of the party named in the order. Therefore, the person or institution on which the order is served must be careful not to inform the named party, otherwise they could commit the offence of tipping off. There are other court orders which can be served under other sections of the Act which will be discussed elsewhere.

There are five orders which can be issued under this part of the Act, namely:

- production order

- search and seizure warrant

- disclosure order

- customer information order

- account monitoring order.

These orders will be granted by a judge following an appropriate application to the court. For a production order in a confiscation investigation or a money laundering investigation the application will be to the Crown Court. For an order in relation to a civil recovery investigation the application must be made to a judge of the High Court. Similar application can be made in Scotland to the Sheriff or the High Court of Justiciary as appropriate.

Let us examine each one in turn:

PRODUCTION ORDERS

Production orders granted under this Act are the same as similar orders under other Acts. These orders require the production of the material specified in the order within seven days beginning with the day on which the order is made. The judge can increase or decrease the time span should it be appropriate. They cover all material including computer records. In the case of computer records they must be made available in a visible and legible form. All such orders not only cover current customers and their records but any former customers.

Although such orders are normally served on the named party for them to produce the required documents, in certain circumstances the judge can issue an order to grant entry. This gives an appropriate officer the right of entry to obtain access to the material.

A production order does not require the person to produce or give access to either privileged or excluded material.[1] Privileged material is any material which the person would be entitled to refuse to produce on grounds of legal professional privilege in proceedings in the High Court. Other than this, a production order has effect in spite of any restriction on disclosure of information no matter how it is imposed. Production orders can be granted to obtain information and material held by government departments.

---

1 Excluded material is defined in the Police and Criminal Evidence Act 1984 (PACE) and includes journalistic material and personal records which are held in confidence.

SEARCH AND SEIZURE WARRANTS

A judge may grant a search and seizure warrant to an appropriate officer if he or she is satisfied that the various conditions laid down in Sections 352 or 353 have been satisfied.

Such a warrant authorises an appropriate person to enter and search the premises specified and to seize and retain any material found there which is likely to be of substantial value, whether or not by itself, to the investigation for the purposes of which the application is made.

For this purpose an appropriate person is a constable or a customs officer if the warrant is sought for the purposes of either a confiscation investigation or a money laundering investigation. In the case of a civil recovery investigation then the appropriate person is a named member of the Asset Recovery Agency.

DISCLOSURE ORDERS

These orders can only be granted on an application made to a judge by the director of the Asset Recovery Agency (see below).

A disclosure order is an order which authorises the director to give notice in writing to any person or organisation which he believes has information or other matter relevant to an investigation, requiring them to do any or all of the following:

- answer questions, either at a time specified in the notice or at once, at a place so specified;

- provide information specified in the notice, by a time and in a manner so specified;

- produce documents, or documents of a description, specified in the notice, either at or by a time so specified or at once, and in a manner so specified.

A disclosure order does not, however, confer any right to require a person to answer any privileged questions, provide any privileged information or produce any privileged document, except that a lawyer may be required to provide the name and address of a client. The definitions and rules regarding what constitutes privileged and excluded material are the same as described above for production orders. Also, such orders have effect in spite of any restriction, however imposed, on the disclosure of information. Details of former customers or of closed accounts are, of course, covered by such orders.

One of the most important things to remember about these orders is that they cannot be obtained or granted in relation to a money laundering investigation. They can only be applied for in confiscation investigation or a civil recovery investigation.

CUSTOMER INFORMATION ORDERS

An application can be made to a judge in the same way and on the same basis as for a production order. Such an order can be obtained by specifying a particular financial institution or institutions or all financial institutions.

If granted, such an order will require the named financial institution or institutions to provide all the information they hold on the person or persons named in the order. What constitutes 'customer information' is extremely wide-ranging and is laid down in Section 364 of the Act. It includes not only the customer's current address but also all previous addresses, as well as the identification evidence taken when the relationship commenced. If the person is a company or similar body then it includes details of the business and any registration details. However, the most wide-ranging aspect of these orders, and to some the most worrying part, is that it also requires the production of information held on other persons or organisations that are not named in the order. This is because the order covers the production of information on any person with whom the named party has a joint account or for any account on which the named party is a signatory. All the information required does not only apply to current customers and their accounts but to all closed accounts and former customers.

To completely understand the requirements of the Act and the breadth of the information required to fully comply with a customer information order, if served on you, it is necessary to study Section 364. This is repeated in full in Appendix 3. As with the other orders, a customer disclosure order has effect in spite of any restriction on the disclosure of information, however imposed.

ACCOUNT MONITORING ORDERS

Here again an application can be made to a judge in the same way and on the same basis as for a production order. An account monitoring order is an order addressed to a financial institution requiring it to provide, for the period stated in the order, information on the account specified to the appropriate officer in the manner and at the times stated in the order. The period stated in the order cannot exceed 90 days beginning with the day on which the order is made.

An account monitoring order, like the others already discussed, has effect in spite of any restriction on the disclosure of information, however imposed.

PART 2 – CONFISCATION

This detailed section covers the whole aspect of the confiscation of property. The two areas which have a direct effect on financial institutions and the question of money laundering relate to restraint orders and confiscation orders.

RESTRAINT ORDERS

Restraint orders can be granted by the Crown Court on an application by the prosecutor, the director of the Asset Recovery Agency or an accredited financial investigator under Sections 40 and 41 of the Act at any time after an investigation has commenced. The order can be granted *ex parte* by a judge in chambers.

A restraint order prohibits the specified persons from dealing in any way with the specified property. Once granted, the order has the effect of freezing the property no matter in whose hands it is in, preventing it from being dealt with or removed from the jurisdiction. The order can be discharged or varied by an application by the person who applied for the order or by the person affected by it.

Financial institutions or others holding property for a person would not normally have the restraint order addressed to or served on them. It will normally be served on the 'owner' of the funds or property and it is in their hands that they are frozen. However, when the party holding the funds or property becomes aware of the order they must freeze them or they could be held to be in contempt of court.

CONFISCATION ORDERS

The Crown Court must issue a confiscation order if two conditions are satisfied. The first is that the defendant has been convicted of an offence in proceedings before the Crown Court or he is committed to the Crown Court for sentencing. The second condition is that the prosecutor (or the director of the Asset Recovery Agency) asks the court to proceed under this section or the court believes it is appropriate for it to do so. The court must decide whether the defendant has a criminal lifestyle. If it is decided he has, then the court must determine whether he has benefited from his general criminal conduct. (If it is decided he does not have a criminal lifestyle, then it must also be decided whether he has benefited from his particular criminal conduct.) If the court decides that the defendant has benefited from such conduct then it must decide the recoverable amount and make a confiscation order requiring him to pay that amount. When making its decisions the court must decide on the balance of probabilities – that is, the civil burden of proof, not the usual criminal one, which is beyond all reasonable doubt.

Most financial institutions or other parties holding property or funds will only become aware of a confiscation order after their customer has been convicted and when there is a request from the customer to pay the funds to the court or a demand from the court for the funds. These funds or property are most likely already subject to a restraint order.

PART 1 – ASSETS RECOVERY AGENCY

Part 1 of the Act sets up the Assets Recovery Agency (the Agency) which is headed up by a director. This Agency is a new concept in UK law and is a new approach in fighting crime.

The aims of the Agency are to disrupt organised crime by removal and recovery of criminal assets either by undertaking direct investigations or assisting other law enforcement agencies. Its other main weapon is the civil recovery proceedings which are taken before the civil courts. For a case to be considered for such action it must have been considered for criminal prosecution which must either have failed or proven impossible to undertake. In addition, the property that could be recovered must be valued at at least £10 000 and must consist of property other than just cash or negotiable securities. The case will, of course, be subject to the normal civil burden of proof; that is, on the balance of probabilities.

In addition, the Agency will undertake any taxation investigation under the Proceeds of Crime Act in those cases where it is believed that there is income or profit on which tax is payable and they are the proceeds of criminal conduct. In such cases the Agency undertakes the functions normally undertaken by HM Revenue and Customs.

All funds and property which the Agency recovers, other than those relating to taxation payments, are paid directly to the Home Office.

BRIBERY AND CORRUPTION

This is not actually part of the Proceeds of Crime Act but is contained in Part 12 of the Anti-terrorism, Crime and Security Act 2001. It is the part of that Act which involves criminal activity other than terrorism, and it has an impact on the Proceeds of Crime Act because of the reporting requirements of criminal conduct. Let us look at what Part 12 says:

Section 108: Bribery and corruption: foreign officers etc.[2]

(1) For the purposes of any common law offence of bribery it is immaterial if the functions of the person who receives or is offered a reward have any connection with the United Kingdom and are carried out in a country or territory outside the United Kingdom.

Section 109: Bribery and corruption committed outside the UK[3]

(1) This section applies if:

(a)   *a national of the United Kingdom or a body incorporated under the law of any part of the United Kingdom does anything in a country or territory outside the United Kingdom, and*

(b)   *the act would, if done in the United Kingdom, constitute a corruption offence (as defined below).*

(2) In such a case:

(a)   *the act constitutes the offence concerned, and*

(b)   *proceedings for the offence may be taken in the United Kingdom.*

So one has to be careful since, if there is any suggestion that a UK national or a UK incorporated body is committing or involved in a form of bribery or corruption outside the UK, this could constitute a criminal offence in the UK. Therefore it would constitute a reportable matter under the Proceeds of Crime Act 2002. Equally, the other offences under that act of 'Concealing etc.', 'Arrangements' or 'Acquisition, use and possession' would also apply.

---

2   Anti-terrorism, Crime and Security Act 2001 – Section 108.
3   Anti-terrorism, Crime and Security Act 2001 – Section 109.

CHAPTER 9

Terrorism Act 2000 – Requirements and Offences

This Act, which consolidated and extended the UK law on terrorism, came into force on 19 February 2001. It is the second of the two pieces of primary UK legislation relating to money laundering. Although this new and comprehensive Act came into force in February 2001 it was very quickly amended by the Anti-terrorism, Crime and Security Act 2001 which was passed following 11 September and came into effect on 14 December 2001.

To understand the money laundering requirements of the Act it is necessary to understand the meaning of terrorism and terrorist property. The Act defines terrorism as the threat of serious violence designed to influence the government or intimidate a section of the public for the purpose of advancing a political, religious or ideological cause. It goes on to define terrorist property as money or other property which is either likely to be used for the purposes of terrorism or the proceeds of an act carried out for the purpose of terrorism. This would obviously include anything which was available for use by a proscribed organisation. The Secretary of State has the power to designate any 'proscribed organisation' as a terrorist organisation. So what are the various offences which can be committed? They are extremely wide-ranging and, like the Proceeds of Crime Act 2002, there are many ways for the unwary to commit an offence. The full details of the offences and the reporting requirements can be found in Appendix 4.

There are two separate reporting requirements in this Act: Section 19 and Section 21A. Section 19 relates to persons and businesses outside the regulated sector, whereas 21A only applies to the regulated sector. The reporting requirements for the regulated sector are basically the same as for the Proceeds of Crime Act; that is, if you know or suspect or there are reasonable grounds for knowing or suspecting then you must report. So in general terms the money laundering requirements and the various court orders that can be served are very similar to, or they have the same effect as, those laid down in the Proceeds of Crime Act. This is why, in practice, most people in the regulated sector, particularly the money laundering reporting officers, make no distinction between them and they treat all money laundering matters in the same way. There is one aspect that needs to be remembered and that involves action overseas. We saw that the Serious Organised Crime and Police Act 2005 amended the Proceeds of Crime Act so that offences have to be offences in both countries. No similar amendment has been made to the Terrorism Act and so the provisions for actions overseas still apply.

This was the position up to 7 July 2005, when the terrorist tube and bus bomb attacks took place in London. The government immediately advised the public that they would be amending the anti-terrorism legislation and that the new laws would be presented to Parliament in October 2005. What these new laws will contain is not yet known but there is no doubt that after the attacks, with the resultant deaths, and the attacks two weeks later, the law is likely to be tightened considerably. Whether this will have any effect on the money laundering and reporting requirements is yet to be seen.

CHAPTER 10

Money Laundering Regulations 2003

The Money Laundering Regulations 2003,[1] which were laid before Parliament on 28 November 2003, implement into UK law the requirements of the Second EU Money Laundering Directive[2] and came into force on 1 March 2004.

The requirements of the Second Directive and how this has extended those of the First Directive were fully discussed in Chapter 4. In this chapter we will consider how those requirements have been introduced and enforced by the 2003 Regulations.

The Regulations comprise four parts.

Part 1 – General

Part 2 – Obligations on persons who carry on relevant business

Part 3 – Money Service Operators and High Value Dealers

Part 4 – Miscellaneous.

Part 1, consisting of Regulations 1 and 2, is mainly concerned with citation, interpretations and definitions; in particular what constitutes 'relevant business'. The definition of 'relevant business' is somewhat long and complex. The full definition is shown in Appendix 1 and must be fully understood by anyone trying to ascertain whether and to what extent they are covered by the Regulations. Such an understanding is vital as failure to comply with the Regulations is a criminal offence which can result in imprisonment.

As already mentioned in Chapters 7 and 9, the introduction of the 2003 Regulations required an amendment to the definition of the regulated sector in both the Proceeds of Crime Act 2002 and the Terrorism Act 2000. This was achieved by two separate statutory instruments, as already described. This extension of the definition of the regulated sector is vital in implementing the requirements of the Second Directive in extending the professions and

---

1   The Money Laundering Regulations 2003 (SI 2003/3075).
2   Directive 2001/97/EC of the European Parliament and of the Council of 4 December 2001.

industries covered by it. However, in order to consider how they are affected it is necessary to consider whether or not they are actually conducting 'relevant business'.

What happens if your business falls within the definition of 'relevant business' and what are the implications? We must look at Part 2 which consists of Regulations 3 to 8. This Part is the one that has the most implications and which applies to the most people. To many people, these are what the Regulations are all about. Indeed, there are those who behave as if these six regulations were 'the Regulations' and forget there are actually 30 with two Schedules. So, if you are conducting a 'relevant business' what must you do? You must establish and maintain:

Regulation 3 – Systems and training to prevent money laundering;

Regulation 4 – Identification procedures;

Regulation 5 – Exceptions to Regulation 4;

Regulation 6 – Record-keeping procedures;

Regulation 7 – Internal reporting procedures; and

Regulation 8 – Casinos' business identification requirements.

A simple look at the first five of these Regulations shows why they are in many respects the most important of the Regulations and the ones that give rise to most of the work and problems. Let us now look at these in detail.

SYSTEMS AND TRAINING TO PREVENT MONEY LAUNDERING (REGULATION 3)[3]

In many ways this can be seen as the most wide-ranging of the Regulations. It requires that every person who is engaged in relevant business within the UK must put in place systems to ensure there is compliance with Regulations 4, 6 and 7. In addition, they must have other procedures of internal control and communications such as are necessary for forestalling and preventing money laundering.

This last requirement is both interesting and worrying as it can be so wide-ranging in its implications. It does not attempt to define what is required and leaves the definition or interpretation of 'appropriate' to the person or

---

3　　Money Laundering Regulations 2003 – Regulation 3.

the Regulators or, ultimately, the courts. In such cases the definition of what is appropriate will be looked at after the event has taken place and with the benefit of hindsight. This makes the planning and implementing of appropriate policies and procedures somewhat difficult and is likely to leave businesses with potential vulnerability.

This Regulation also requires that all relevant businesses ensure that they take appropriate measures so that all relevant employees are made aware of the provisions of the Regulations and also of Part 7 of the Proceeds of Crime Act 2002 and of Sections 18 and 21A of the Terrorism Act 2000. Such training must also include how to recognise and deal with transactions that may be related to money laundering.

This training requirement is extensive, particularly as there is no definition of who are 'relevant employees'. Businesses should review their activities and their employees to ensure that they train all necessary staff. As the law stands, it may not be necessary to train all employees, but how do you decide which require such training? Perhaps the best guidance available is that given in the Joint Money Laundering Steering Group Guidance Notes, which suggest that:

> To safeguard a firm's reputational and regulatory position, it is recommended that all directors, senior management and staff, regardless of whether they are handling relevant financial business, have access to information concerning their personal statutory responsibilities and those of the firm.[4]

Training has now become one of the most important aspects of ensuring compliance with the increasing legislation and regulations. Such legislation and regulations, including those made by the appropriate regulators, have become so complex that without training employees can easily leave both themselves as individuals and their employers vulnerable to serious potential criminal sanction.

New employees will obviously be in immediate need of comprehensive training, not only in the law and regulations but also in their employer's internal controls and procedures. The training is not a one-off exercise but must be seen as an ongoing process, and employees must be made aware of both any changes to the firm's procedures and any changes to the law and regulations. How do you carry out this necessary training? Firms must consider all the various different types, such as face-to-face, videos or e-learning. There is no

---

4   JMLSG Guidance Notes, paragraph 6.5.

right and wrong way. Much will depend on the size and composition of the firm concerned. E-learning has many advantages, such as avoiding the need to take employees away from their workplace for a long time or in large numbers. It can be tailored to meet the firm's needs and easily updated and amended as the procedures, regulations or law changes.

No matter which system is used, the firm must ensure that it maintains sufficient training records for all employees to be able to demonstrate their compliance with the 2003 Regulations.

Failure to comply with the Regulations is a criminal offence punishable by a term of up to two years' imprisonment or a fine. It is a defence to show that all reasonable steps were taken and that all due diligence was exercised in putting in place systems and training.

IDENTIFICATION PROCEDURES (REGULATION 4)[5]

This Regulation is probably the one that is the most commonly known and spoken about. It is also the one that gives the most problems and cause for concern. It is also the basis of most of the complaints about the practical operation of the whole money laundering requirements.

This procedure is most frequently called 'know your customer (client)' (KYC) although sometimes it is also referred to as 'customer (client) due diligence' (CDD). It is the fundamental basis of customer relationships and is also the basis on which compliance with the money laundering legislation is built. It is often said that there are three parts to the KYC process: first, to satisfy yourself that the prospective customer is who they claim to be; second, to ascertain the nature of the proposed relationship; and third, to obtain enough information about the proposed customer's business so as to ascertain the legitimacy of the relationship.

However, this is all at the beginning of the relationship and is all part of the identification and verification of the new customer and is therefore only the first part of KYC. Full KYC is, arguably, a much longer-term affair and is effectively a 'cradle to grave' requirement. That is, to be truly effective and useful it is necessary for KYC to be an ongoing matter to keep the profile of customers up-to-date and accurate, which is consistent with the recommendations of FATF which make it clear that ongoing due diligence is necessary.

5　　Money Laundering Regulations 2003 – Regulation 4.

So, what do the Regulations actually say and require? Basically if you are to carry out 'relevant business' within the UK then you must, as soon as is reasonably practicable, after your first contact with the potential client, obtain from them satisfactory evidence of their identity. The establishment of identity must be undertaken if any of the following circumstances occur:

- two or more parties agree, or form, a business relationship;

- if you know or suspect that a one-off transaction involves money laundering;

- in respect of a one-off transaction for €15 000 or more;

- in respect of two or more one-off transactions which appear to be linked and total €15 000 or more.

In the above, a 'business relationship' is defined as 'any arrangement the purpose of which is to facilitate the carrying on of transactions on a frequent, habitual or regular basis where the total amount of any payments to be made by any person to any other in the course of the arrangement is not known or capable of being ascertained at the outset',[6] while a one-off transaction is defined as 'any transaction other than one carried out in the course of an existing business relationship'.[7]

Where the applicant for business or client is apparently acting for a third party then reasonable steps must be taken to identify that third party. If there is more than one applicant it will be necessary to decide whether or not to identify all the applicants. The JMLSG Guidance Notes state:

> Firms may wish to decide that all relevant parties to the relationship should be identified at the outset. In addition, firms should remember that identification is only one anti-money laundering tool, so where identification exemptions apply or, where there is no duty to identify, firms are still required to have in place adequate overall anti-money laundering risk management control.[8]

It is clear that obtaining evidence of identity of every client is a vital start to any relationship and that the transaction must not take place before satisfactory identification has been obtained. Failure to establish identity may constitute a criminal offence which can be punishable by two years' imprisonment, a fine,

---

6   Money Laundering Regulations 2003 – Regulation 2(1).
7   Money Laundering Regulations 2003 – Regulation 2(1).
8   JMLSG Guidance Notes, paragraph 4.6.

or both. However, does this requirement apply to each and every client, or are there any exceptions? There are a number of exceptions and these are detailed in Regulation 5 which is discussed below and full details of which appear in Appendix 2. These exceptions, while relatively narrow, are important and must be fully understood.

EXCEPTIONS (REGULATION 5)

While everyone talks about Regulation 4 and the identification requirements, they can often overlook the exceptions. The full details of the Regulation can be found in Appendix 2. The exceptions mainly revolve around other authorised firms. However, the Regulation does need careful consideration to avoid undertaking identity checks when not necessary or, more importantly, not undertaking checks when required.

RECORD-KEEPING (REGULATION 6)

This is also a very important regulation which has major practical implications. The requirements and implications are fully discussed in Chapter 13.

INTERNAL REPORTING PROCEDURES (REGULATION 7)

This Regulation sets out the need for the establishment of an internal reporting system. Under this Regulation an organisation, other than a sole practitioner, must appoint a person nominated to receive internal reports. These requirements apply to all firms or organisations subject to the Money Laundering Regulations 2003. They are, of course, supplemented and expanded upon by the FSA in its Money Laundering Sourcebook in respect of firms regulated by the FSA. These requirements and the practical problems are discussed in Chapter 14.

CASINOS (REGULATION 8)[9]

This Regulation relates solely to casinos, which were brought within the money laundering requirements by the Second EU Directive. It also only relates to their requirements to identify those using gaming facilities. The whole Regulation is as follows:

---

9   Money Laundering Regulations 2003 – Regulation 8.

8.

(1) A person who operates a casino by way of business in the United Kingdom must obtain satisfactory evidence of identity of any person before allowing that person to use the casino's gaming facilities.

(2) A person who fails to do so is to be treated as having contravened Regulation 3.

So, having looked in this chapter at the various legal and regulatory requirements involved in the Money Laundering Regulations 2003, let us turn in Chapter 11 to some of the practical implications and problems.

How to Implement in Practice the UK Anti-Money Laundering Legislation and Regulations – General Review

In previous chapters we have discussed the legal and regulatory requirements of the UK and the international initiatives which have affected and influenced it. In the next chapters we are going to consider how these requirements can be implemented in practice and the problems which can arise.

The tendency is to assume that money laundering offences and requirements only apply to those in the 'regulated sector', but of course this is incorrect. For example, the principal money laundering offences set out in Sections 327 to 329 of the Proceeds of Crime Act 2002 can be committed by, or affect, anyone. Other sections of the Act and the Terrorism Act 2000 contain similar offences and requirements. However, the day-to-day fight against money laundering, and ensuring compliance with the various laws and regulations, does fall firmly onto the 'regulated sector'. The actions and procedures that they must follow will be discussed in the following chapters.

The law and regulations, coupled with rules issued by regulators, are complex, to say the least, as well as in some ways contradictory, and are subject to interpretation. Therein lies the problems in implementation and ensuring their requirements are met. None of the laws or regulations really state how you should comply, merely that you must. To help, some industry bodies have produced guidance notes on how to comply. The first and most comprehensive are those issued by the Joint Money Laundering Steering Group (JMLSG). They cover the whole of the UK financial sector. They were first issued in 1990 and have since been revised and updated. The latest review took place in 2004 and the proposed revisions were issued for consultation in March 2005. This consultation was scheduled to be completed by the end of June 2005. It is then hoped for them to be agreed and issued for implementation at the end of 2005 or early 2006.

These guidance notes have had a tremendous influence on anti-money laundering procedures as they have been used not only by other UK sectors in drafting their guidance notes but have also been used by many other countries around the world as the blueprint for their guidance notes, some of which are issued by their regulators. The other, more important, consideration is that to date the JMLSG Guidance Notes have been approved by HM Treasury. This is important because industry guidance notes approved by HM Treasury must be taken into consideration by a judge in any court case. This is important in the defence of anyone accused of an offence under the Money Laundering Regulations. The revised JMLSG Guidance Notes mentioned above should be similarly approved once the consultation period is complete.

So let us now look in detail at the main problem areas and the practical issues in meeting the requirements. In reality, the whole of a business's operation and procedures are affected by the requirements.

CULTURE

This may seem a strange place to start but in any question of how any organisation sets and meets its compliance and regulatory responsibilities the overall culture of the organisation is paramount. All organisations have a culture that determines how they operate. This culture covers all aspects of the business and is fundamental in how it sets its policies, structures and principles and then how these are implemented via its procedures and operations. This culture has to be set and implemented from the top. It goes from the chairperson of the board downwards, not from junior staff upwards. The whole question of complying with the various anti-money laundering laws and regulations has now become such a fundamental part of any business in the regulated sector that it now has to be a fundamental part of the culture. Without this it will not be taken seriously by all employees or be absorbed into all aspects of everyday operational systems and procedures. This becomes even more vital if a firm is to adopt the risk-based approach which is likely to be the preferred way to successfully handle anti-money laundering requirements, and is now being fully advocated by the Financial Services Authority (FSA). It is also in line with FATF Recommendation 5 and the Basel CDD paper (see Chapter 2).

POLICIES AND PROCEDURES

From an organisation's culture we can then devise policies which lead directly to the creation of the procedures. In other words, the firm must devise its policies so that it meets all its legal and regulatory requirements while at the same time ensuring it can meet all its customer and business commitments.

The policies must cover:

- know your customer (KYC)
- know your business (KYB)
- reporting requirements
- money laundering reporting officer and their duties/responsibilities
- handling court orders
- tipping off
- record-keeping
- employee awareness and training.

KNOW YOUR CUSTOMER/CLIENT (KYC)

When you speak to most people, both within and outside the regulated sector, the main thing they think about is KYC. This is one of the major aspects of anti-money laundering compliance and the area which gives the main concern. This important topic is discussed in detail in Chapter 12.

KNOW YOUR BUSINESS (KYB)

Everyone has heard of KYC and it is now part and parcel of all businesses within the regulated sector. However, you also need to understand the principles of KYB, which is equally important if you are to fulfil your money laundering responsibilities. So what do we mean by this expression? Let us list some of the important questions you need to consider.

- What type of business, product or service do you normally undertake and handle?
- How do you normally handle the above?
- Size or frequency of business?
- What is your normal way of doing business (face-to-face or remotely)?

- Is there a geographical basis to your business and/or customers?

- What type of customer or client do you normally have?

- How are you normally approached by customers?

This list is not comprehensive but points out various aspects that you need to think about. Knowledge of your business linked to the typologies, national and international findings is vital in ensuring that you have all the necessary policies and procedures in place. They will also assist when coupled with KYC information in assessing a suspicious activity or transaction.

RECORD-KEEPING

However you handle the regulatory and legal requirements of money laundering, whether in the major areas of KYC, monitoring, suspicion reporting, handling court orders, training or any other area, the most important thing is to ensure that full and proper records are kept. It must, of course, be remembered that there is nothing in the money laundering legislation or the FSA rules that requires the retention of original documents. These requirements are more fully discussed in Chapter 13.

REPORTING REQUIREMENTS

This is frequently one of the most contentious parts of the legislation. In Chapter 14 we will discuss the details of the reporting requirements and how to handle this important and difficult subject. As we have already seen, for the regulated sector, a requirement is to report when you have knowledge, suspicion or there are reasonable grounds for knowledge or suspicion. There is also the problem of obtaining consent when your knowledge or suspicion occurs prior to the transaction being undertaken. One always has to remember that making a report to the NCIS is frequently only the start of the matter. There are many occasions when your problems only start after a report is made to the NCIS. One of the problems that can arise after reporting is tipping off, as mentioned earlier, but the other main one, which has nothing to do with money laundering, is that of constructive trust.

THE ROLE OF THE MONEY LAUNDERING REPORTING OFFICER

The money laundering reporting officer (MLRO) is now one of the most important positions in the whole of the anti-money laundering framework, particularly for firms regulated by the FSA. Chapter 15 covers the responsibilities and role of this officer and the duties and other areas they are now responsible for.

THE MONEY LAUNDERING REPORTING OFFICER'S ANNUAL REPORT

This report is required under the FSA Sourcebook for all FSA-regulated firms. It is required at least annually. Full details of what is required and its implications are discussed in Chapter 16.

EMPLOYEE AWARENESS AND TRAINING

The current law and regulations in the UK have been enhanced by the FSA Sourcebook. They require that all employees who could, in any way, be involved in the handling (or are managerially responsible for the handling) of transactions which may involve money laundering receive adequate training. Failure to provide this could leave employers in danger of both committing a criminal offence and breaching regulatory requirements. For those firms regulated by the FSA, the MLRO is responsible for the satisfaction of this important matter (see also Chapter 17).

To be successful, anti-money laundering requirements should be seen as the 'right thing to do' and part of good business governance. Regrettably, a study published in June 2005 showed that, in the UK at least, this was far from the actual situation. This study, titled 'Anti-money Laundering Requirements: Costs, Benefits and Perceptions' was written by Z/Yen Ltd and published by the Corporation of London in association with the Institute of Chartered Accountants in England and Wales as part of the City Research Series.

The results of this study are of concern, as regards the perception of UK businesses and professions compared to their international counterparts. The study shows that when asked how practical anti-money laundering regulations were to implement, 75 per cent of UK accountants and 84 per cent of UK lawyers felt they were 'impractical' or 'very impractical'. However, the same questions asked of international accountants and lawyers gave answers of 39 per cent and 33 per cent respectively. This is a worrying situation if perceptions in the UK appear to be so different from those in other parts of the world.

Turning to other professions and businesses, the pattern seems to be the same. Almost two-thirds of UK respondents in the study said that anti-money laundering regulations were too severe in proportion to the risks of money laundering, while only one-third of international respondents felt this way. Overall, UK-based companies comply with AMLR[1] in order to avoid sanctions from the authorities, not because they perceive AMLR as representing good business practice or as being effective at combating money laundering. Of international respondents, 51 per cent believed complying was both the right thing to do and good business practice. Figure 11.1 shows the statistics in the study with the reasons for complying.

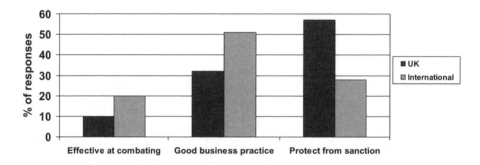

Figure 11.1   Reasons for complying with AMLR

The costs of complying were also considered to be much higher in the UK than in other major countries. The UK costs are said to be 25 per cent higher than in the USA, over double those in Germany and almost three times those in France and Italy.

The results of this important study show that there is an urgent need to review costs and benefits, and also to change the perception of the effectiveness of anti-money laundering measures and impress upon companies the importance of undertaking them.

Unless the corporate culture accepts the need for these measures and that effective anti-money laundering requirements are not only the 'right thing to do' but also good business practice, there will be continuing difficulty in implementing the requirements effectively. While the costs and effectiveness must be examined, and amended where necessary, it is the culture of many parts of UK society that needs to change if the fight against money laundering and terrorist financing is to be won.

---

1   Anti-Money Laundering Regulations.

CHAPTER 12

Know Your Customer (KYC)

As we discussed in Chapter 11, when you speak to most people, both within and outside the regulated sector, the main thing they think about is KYC. For the general public it is really the only area of the money laundering regulations that they come into contact with. It is also the one that is frequently misunderstood by the general public and even employees within the regulated sector. In addition, to many people KYC only means the process of identification and verification of a new customer or client (that is, ID&V). This, of course, is not just the case. ID&V is the start of the KYC process. KYC is therefore essential not only to identify your new customers but also to ensure that you do not establish any relationship with anyone who is on a UN sanction list or the similar list issued by the Bank of England.

WHAT IS A CUSTOMER?

To start with, we need to define what we mean by a customer and when they need to be identified. The term customer does not actually appear in the Regulations;[1] they refer to identifying an 'applicant for business' which is defined as 'a person seeking to form a business relationship, or carry out a one-off transaction, with another person acting in the course of relevant business[2] carried on by that other person in the UK'.

The same Regulation defines a 'business relationship' as:

> any arrangement the purpose for which is to facilitate the carrying out of transactions on a frequent, habitual or regular basis where the total amount of any payments to be made by any person to any other in the course of the arrangement is not known or capable of being ascertained at the outset.

Clearly, this definition does not include one-off transactions; however, a relationship need not involve a transaction. The giving of advice may constitute establishing a business relationship.

---

1   Money Laundering Regulations 2003 – Regulation 2.
2   See Appendix 1.

So now we have defined who is a customer for the purposes of carrying out ID&V when the relationship is established. However, as shown earlier, KYC goes much further than simply knowing your customer when you first establish the relationship; true KYC covers the relationship from 'cradle to grave'. In other words, it is knowing your customer throughout the relationship and keeping your knowledge up-to-date over the whole life of that relationship. Of course, this is easier said than done, and the lengths taken will obviously vary from industry to industry according to the risk involved. The risk aspect of KYC has only relatively recently been considered. The Financial Services Authority (FSA) has now made it clear that the financial sector should consider and handle KYC on a risk-based approach. A risk-based approach is also in line with the FATF Recommendations.

HOW DO YOU UNDERTAKE ID&V?

Let us now look at how to undertake ID&V and why it is essential. As mentioned above, the legislation and money laundering regulations are not much help. They tell you that you must identify new customers but they do not tell you how or indeed what information you need. Even the FSA does not actually say how to do it, only that you must. The 'how' has been left to the various industries to come up with their own guidance notes, as mentioned in Chapter 6. The JMLSG Guidance Notes are the most widely used, representing the whole financial sector, and are signed off by the Treasury. We will take a quick look at what they say and what is being proposed in the 2005 consultation exercise.

What does the identification of customers consist of, how does it usually take place and what does it entail? Generally the JMLSG Guidance Notes lay down the systems, procedures and recommendations to follow, even for people not in the financial sector.

Let us look at individuals first, and remind ourselves that the information you are collecting and verifying is not only to meet your regulatory responsibilities but to establish knowledge of your customer for your future business relationship. Without this base knowledge, how can you be sure that you are providing the most appropriate service to your customer and sell them the most relevant products for their needs? What information do you need to identify your customer? The basic information you need to obtain for each individual new customer is:

- customer's full name and address

- date of birth

- nationality

- country of residence.

Having obtained that information you need to see (for each individual) and retain records/copies of a document of identification such as a passport or driving licence to verify their name, and a separate document to confirm their address. This second document may be a utility bill, bank statement or some other official document. While this at first sounds simple and straightforward, there are problems. A driving licence is not actually a 'document of identification' and, even if it were, not everyone in the UK has a driving licence. The number of people holding a passport is even lower. In practice, therefore, there are many people who do not hold one of the normally accepted identification documents. Herein lies one of the main practical problems in satisfying the regulatory requirements. Without an official identification document in the UK and with many people not holding one of the normally accepted documents many people find it hard to prove their identity. When you add this to a basic reluctance by many people to provide identification which is, in their view, contrary to their freedom and culture of the UK where, until recently, no one had to prove who they were, the problems in meeting the regulatory requirements are clear.

These raise a whole series of practical problems. Since many people cannot produce the normally accepted documents, financial institutions have to try to achieve a measure of compliance by using other documents or forms of identifying potential customers. This is where the guidance notes are of great use as they suggest documents which could be used. However, nothing takes away from the institution concerned the fact it must satisfy itself as to the identity of all its clients. There is also the question of those who, because of their lack of identification documentation due, for example, to their legal or physical inability, their dependence on others or other financial difficulties, could become financially or socially excluded. If a potential customer genuinely cannot provide any or only part of the normal identification documentation then the institution must have in place policies and procedures to prevent such exclusion. This can be achieved by means other than the standard identification methods. If they do establish a relationship in these circumstances then they will need to take what identification they can and then must clearly document the reasons for their decision to proceed with the relationship. Care must always be taken when considering establishing a relationship with students or young people. They must not automatically be considered as falling into the category of financially or socially excluded. Many hold passports and can satisfy the standard identification procedures.

This always supposes that you are dealing with the customer in a face-to-face environment but today more and more relationships are established and future business conducted remotely, for example on the Internet. Indeed, many institutions never actually meet their customers at all. So how do you achieve satisfactory identification and verification in a totally remote environment? You could request customers to send you copies of documents, but these will need to be confirmed and verified in some way. Simply taking copies sent by the customer proves nothing; they could be false or altered. The best way is to use the various electronic checks which are increasingly available through credit reference agencies and similar companies, and use the ever increasing data held electronically on everyone. To be effective and acceptable for the ID&V process, the data must be obtained from more than one source or database. This is becoming easier and more commonplace. However, doing all this remotely requires the use of additional checks to mitigate the greater potential for money laundering or impersonation and fraud. Such electronic checks can also be used to identify or verify face-to-face contacts, particularly when not all the usual documents are available. It is in this situation that a good risk assessment procedure needs to be put in place. You must risk-assess all products so as to identify and differentiate between those that have a low money laundering risk and those with a greater risk potential. If the product is considered to be low risk then the standard identification of the customer, discussed above, should be sufficient. However, the higher the risk assessment of the product, the more additional identification and verification checks must be made.

This shows the need to operate on a risk-based approach and not treat all customers the same. The FSA has made it clear this is the way it considers the financial sector should go. The 2005 proposed revision of the JMLSG Guidance Notes is designed to encourage firms to adopt risk-based policies for the purposes of money laundering including terrorist financing. Such policies should also clearly emphasise senior management's responsibility for these policies and their implementation. Introducing such an approach is not easy and will depend not only on the products supplied but the firm's operational and corporate structure. However the assessment is undertaken, it must be done in such a way as to enable a company to accurately assess the risks posed by not only the different customers and products but any combination of them as well. It must also cover the verification which must be applied to each level of risk posed by that customer. It must also always be kept in mind that these assessments and profiles are not static but will change not only with alterations in the customer's profile but also with changes in the threat assessment as money launderers use different methods.

POLITICALLY EXPOSED PERSONS (PEPs)

The amount of corruption and abuse of public funds by some government leaders and public officials over recent years has given great cause for concern both internationally as well as in the countries involved. These people are collectively known as politically exposed persons or PEPs. It is argued that these people are different from other customers because of the size of the illegal funds that can be involved and also the high public profile that will result if things go wrong and mistakes are found.

PEPs are defined as:

> *Individuals who are or have been entrusted with prominent public functions, including heads of state or government, senior politicians, senior government, judicial or military officials, senior executives of publicly owned corporations and important political party officials.*[3]

This definition extends to cover not only the individual but also their family, close associates and any businesses they have a relationship with. Clearly it is not always easy to identify whether the individual or any of the legal entities should be classified as PEPs. One of the options is to turn to lists of potential PEPs published by commercial or official authorities. Having a PEP status does not automatically incriminate the person or any of their transactions. It does, however, put them into a higher risk category which will need to be taken into account in any risk-based approach.

Firms must have in place the necessary procedures to carry out the necessary additional due diligence, including measures to establish source of wealth and source of funds.

Most firms have such procedures in place to recognise anyone who falls into the PEP category when they approach them to establish a relationship. However, what about customers who have already been accepted and have an established relationship before they become a PEP? Firms must also have in place systems and procedures to identify existing customers whose profiles change to fall within the PEP definition, and then undertake any necessary

---

3   Basel Committee Customer Due Diligence paper, published in October 2001.

additional due diligence. This is an area where many firms fall down, but this can and should be achieved if firms carry out a full KYC procedure.

So having considered the ID&V for personal customers, let us turn to non-personal relationships. The ID&V requirements for these customers are similar to those for personal customers, with certain additions. First, you need to identify the firm as an entity and then each of the owners, partners and directors should be named as individuals in the manner already discussed. To identify the firm you need to obtain:

- its full name

- its legal status (for example, partnership, private company, public company)

- where it is incorporated

- both its registered and operational addresses

- the type of business (what business is it in)

- names of all directors, partners and so on.

This information should be verified from appropriate public records or documents produced. Having obtained this information, how much further it is necessary to take the verification process will depend upon the risk-based approach of the institution. For example, if dealing with a publicly quoted company which is subject to all the normal public disclosure rules, it may be unnecessary to undertake any further verification. However, if it is a private company then verification of the directors and/or shareholders will be required.

For partnerships, unincorporated businesses, charities, clubs and so on the same basic principles apply. These types of businesses vary tremendously in size, type of business and risk involved. These are areas where the institution needs to have a fully operational risk assessment procedure in place. These are relationships which can result in increased problems and greater risk, so extra care needs to be exercised.

There are also situations when relationships with other regulated firms or public sector bodies are being established. Here, although you need to satisfy yourself that the potential customer is who they say they are and is properly regulated, the standard identification requirements are not necessary.

The above comments on ID&V only cover the basic principles. To cover them in detail it would be necessary to repeat most of the JMLSG Guidance Notes. The important point is that an institution must follow whatever guidance notes relate to its industry and then ensure that it has comprehensive, risk-based, fully operational and compliant with policies in place that have been fully approved by the senior management.

So far, we have discussed the question of ID&V – in other words, the start of the KYC process when establishing a relationship. However, as we said at the beginning of this chapter, KYC goes much further than this, so let us now turn to the question of ongoing KYC once a relationship has been established.

ONGOING KYC

The concept of ongoing KYC covers all aspects of a customer's affairs. What needs to be collected, when and how often will be dependent on the customer concerned and the risk assessments you have made. The other important aspect is, of course, whether the operations and transactions being seen are actually in line with the current profile. Most of the information you need is the same as you would wish to obtain for standard business considerations. It can be obtained either during business meetings or from other information that comes into your possession. One of the other important triggers that indicates a need to revise a customer's profile occurs as a result of monitoring transactions as part of the procedure for suspicion reporting, as examined in Chapter 14. The highlighting of a transaction during this process could indicate suspicious activity or that the customer profile, and hence the KYC, is not up-to-date. You must use whatever information, facts or knowledge you can to keep your customer's profile current. This helps you to satisfy a number of requirements. It will help in ensuring that your knowledge of your customer is up-to-date as well as enabling you to offer them the best products and services. It will indicate when there is a need to change or reconsider the risk profile of that customer. Finally, if you are using a computer-based monetary system (often called an Intelligent Transactional Monitoring system), an accurate profile of the customer is essential if the system is to work properly and you are to get the best results from it. KYC therefore covers several needs and, if carried out thoroughly, will enable you to comply with your statutory and regulatory responsibility as well as provide your customer with the best service possible.

CHAPTER 13

Record-keeping

Of all the various money laundering requirements, record-keeping might seem the most mundane and least important. How wrong can you be? Record-keeping is a fundamental part of the whole anti-money laundering regime and without it many of the requirements cannot be met. The record-keeping requirements in respect of identification and verification (ID&V) evidence and transactional records are contained in Regulation 6[1] while the FSA rules[2] cover other aspects. The regulations do not specify where or how records should be kept, only that the firm must be able to retrieve information without undue delay. Another important point that needs to be remembered is that, notwithstanding the time limits set by the Money Laundering Regulations 2003, the records relating to an ongoing investigation should be retained until confirmation is received from the law enforcement agency involved stating that the case is closed. This, of course, means that once a firm is aware of an investigation it must ensure that none of the appropriate records are destroyed under the firm's normal archive destruction timetable.

A breach of any of the record-keeping requirements can result in prosecution and/or regulatory sanction. Indeed, many firms have found themselves in trouble with their regulators because of their poor record-keeping.

Let us look first at the records that must be kept in respect of the ID&V of new customers. The regulations require that, where evidence has been obtained, by way of identifying anyone establishing a business relationship, then copies of that evidence (or information as to where a copy may be obtained) must be kept for a period of not less than five years from the date when the relationship ceases. We have already seen the problems of obtaining this evidence and now we can see the second practical problem. How do you keep and record such evidence when, at the time it is obtained, you have no idea how long you are going to have to keep it? This problem is particularly troublesome to those firms whose records are all kept in paper form, and will only get worse as the years progress and requirements remain unchanged. Let us take a simple example which, while it may be a little extreme, is not impossible with the general increase in life expectancy.

---

1   Money Laundering Regulations 2003.
2   Financial Services Authority Money Laundering Sourcebook.

A woman opens an account with a bank at the age of 18 when going to university. She is happy with her bank and maintains her account with them until her death at the age of 93. The bank will have to maintain her ID&V records for the 75 years the account was open plus five years after closure; that is, a total of 80 years. The practical problem of keeping these records is clear, and one of the most difficult ones to overcome. One does have to ask whether keeping copies of a gas bill for 80 years will actually achieve a great deal. Still, while the regulations stand, we must find ways of complying with them. Obviously there is no need to keep records in paper format, and one of the best ways of dealing with this problem is to consider an electronic system into which all evidence documents can be scanned. Today, more and more ID&V is being done electronically but even then the requirements of Regulation 6 fully apply, with the need to produce the 'evidence' if required.

On occasion, the ID&V requirements may be carried out overseas on a firm's behalf. If that happens, then the firm must be satisfied that there is no legal restriction to the evidence being made available on demand. If there is any doubt, due to such things as Data Protection legislation or any privacy laws, then copies of the identification evidence must be requested at the time it is taken by the overseas institution. If they cannot provide it at that time then it cannot be considered that they have undertaken satisfactory ID&V and it will have to be achieved in some other way. If documents are retained overseas then the firm must take appropriate action to ensure that the record retention policy in the country concerned matches that of the UK so that the documents can be produced as required under UK law if necessary.

Turning now to transactional records; the Regulations require that a firm must record all transactions carried out on behalf of or with a customer in the course of relevant business. Transaction records in support of entries in the accounts, in whatever form they are used, should be kept so as to form an audit trail which will establish a financial profile of any suspect account or customer. These requirements are therefore straightforward, and in line with most normal business practice. Indeed in many industries and firms such records are kept for longer periods.

The FSA, in Section 7 of its Money Laundering Sourcebook, also requires that all regulated firms make and retain records of all internal reports to the money laundering reporting officer (MLRO) and external reports to the National Criminal Intelligence Service (NCIS). If the MLRO has not passed an internal report to the NCIS he or she must keep a record of both that report and all other material considered in making the decision.

There is also a requirement to keep records of all employee awareness and training. These records should show the employee's name, the date, the training given and the results of any test. Records must also be retained of each report made by the MLRO to the senior management together with records of their consideration and what action they took on receipt of the report. All these records required by the FSA should be kept and be retrievable for a period of at least five years from the date they were created.

To achieve all these various requirements, the firm must have a document retention policy. Firms, particularly those in the financial sector, must weigh the statutory and regulatory requirements, together with the needs of the law enforcement authorities, against the normal commercial considerations including the cost of maintaining large archives.

It must be remembered that the above record-keeping requirements are the minimum necessary, as laid down in the Second EU Directive and the Money Laundering Regulations 2003. There may be other legal, regulatory or operational demands that require such records to be kept for longer periods.

CHAPTER 14

Reporting Requirements

In Chapter 7 we discussed in detail the reporting requirements of the Proceeds of Crime Act 2002 for those working in the regulated sector. Similar requirements under the Terrorism Act 2000 were covered in Chapter 9. From a practical point of view, the Acts are similar in terms of their reporting and so here we will consider them as one.

WHEN TO REPORT

What reporting is necessary under this important aspect of the money laundering requirements? First, anyone in the regulated sector who knows or suspects, or where there are reasonable grounds for knowing or suspecting from information or other sources which come to them in the course of their business, that another person is engaged in money laundering then they *must* report it. This report should be made to the firm's 'nominated officer'. In a FSA-regulated firm this is usually the money laundering reporting officer (MLRO) and we will use this title for the rest of our discussions in this chapter. All this sounds reasonably straightforward; but here are some of the practical problems.

KNOWLEDGE

First, what are 'knowledge' and 'suspicion'? Taking knowledge first, it sounds simple but its definition has been subject to discussion. Perhaps the easiest definition to take is that used in the JMLSG 2003 Guidance Notes[1] which simply defines knowledge as 'actual knowledge'. Unfortunately the legal definition is more complicated. Knowledge has been defined for the purpose of civil law by *Baden Delvaux* v. *Société Général* 1992[2] to include the following:

- wilfully shutting one's mind to the obvious;

- wilfully and recklessly failing to make such enquiries as a reasonable and honest person would make;

---

1   Joint Money Laundering Steering Group Guidance Notes, 2003 edition.
2   [1993] 1 W.L.R. 509.

- knowledge of the circumstances which would indicate facts to an honest and reasonable person;

- knowledge of the circumstances which would put an honest and reasonable person on enquiry.

No matter how knowledge is defined, this information must come to the person in the course of their professional activities.

SUSPICION

Over the years, 'suspicion' has been defined by the courts as being beyond mere speculation and based upon some foundation; that is, 'a degree of satisfaction and not necessarily amounting to belief but at least extending beyond speculation as to whether an event has occurred or not'; and 'although the creation of suspicion requires a lesser factual basis than the creation of a belief, it must nonetheless be built upon some foundation'.

A further example is Lord Devlin in the Court of Appeal decision in *Hussein* v. *Chong Fook Kam*:[3] 'Suspicion in its ordinary meaning is a state of conjecture or surmise where proof is lacking: I suspect but I cannot prove.' Such definitions are, of course, subjective. However, the current legislation does not only mention pure knowledge and suspicion, both of which are difficult to prove in court, but goes on to include 'reasonable grounds'.

What does this actually mean? The UK courts have yet to test the concept of 'reasonable grounds to know or suspect'. However, from an examination of the Hansard Reports on the Parliamentary debates on what was then the Proceeds of Crime Bill it is clear that Parliament meant it to include both negligence and also wilful blindness; which leads us to the question of what is wilful blindness? This can be simply defined as 'the intentional and deliberate avoidance of the facts'. So, taking all this into consideration it is likely that the courts will determine reasonable grounds as existing when it can be demonstrated that there are facts or circumstances from which a reasonable person engaged in a business subject to the Money Laundering Regulations would have inferred knowledge, or formed the suspicion, that another person was engaged in money laundering.

---

3   1 [1970] AC 942.

HOW TO REPORT

Thus, having reviewed *when* you report, *how* is this achieved in practice? Whatever measures you take to recognise knowledge, suspicion or reasonable grounds, knowledge of your customer is a key requirement: in other words, the key to recognising a reportable transaction is KYC.

To meet their obligations, most firms set up various types of monitoring systems to check their transactions against what is known about their customer and at the same time against the profile of previous transactions or deals. This is an area which tends to generate the majority of reports currently submitted to the National Criminal Intelligence Service (NCIS). This monitoring can be undertaken in any number of ways, and how it is done depends on the structure of a firm as well as its size. Most larger firms, and indeed many medium-sized ones, have implemented the use of computer-based systems usually referred to as Intelligent Transactional Monitoring systems. Such systems are highly effective and allow the MLRO to use their scarce resources in those areas which are seen as highest risk. However, for these systems to work effectively they have to have full access to all a firm's systems and records together with all national and international findings and all other intelligence available. It is important that the firm's KYC policies and procedures are fully implemented and kept up-to-date, and that all the records are accurate. However, no matter how good the Intelligent Transaction Monitoring system is, it cannot give you correct 'answers'. It cannot identify 'money laundering transactions'; it can only highlight those transactions that are out of the ordinary or meet certain predetermined criteria. The transactions highlighted must then be fully investigated before you can satisfy yourself as to the genuineness of the transaction or decide that you are suspicious and hence need to report.

Of course, it is not just a question of transactions that do not meet the norm; it can also be an unusual or out of the ordinary use of products or services, which would include business operations that do not appear to have any commercial rationale. The type of situation which may be unusual and which in certain circumstances might give rise to reasonable grounds for suspicion varies depending on the institution concerned and their customer or transactional base. In their 2003 edition of their Guidance Notes, the JMLSG produce a lengthy list of illustrations of types of situations which could give rise to suspicion. These could apply to any firm within the financial sector or elsewhere. This list, together with the various typologies produced by FATF and also similar lists produced by NCIS, should be used to produce filters or similar methods of assessing suspicion. They must, of course, be kept current and amended as necessary. These lists and filters, while important, are not the only ways of becoming suspicious. We must always remember that it is not only transactions but also the surrounding circumstances, actions or situations which can give rise to suspicion.

Having now looked at knowledge and suspicion, we should look at how and when you report, which is one of the main practical problems. The Regulations and, where appropriate, the FSA Rules, lay down the need to set up an internal reporting system to the MLRO. How such a system operates will again depend upon the size, structure and geographical spread of a firm. Whatever the system, the basics must be the same – that all employees know what, how and to whom they must report. It is also essential that the reporting lines from the person with the suspicion and the MLRO are as short and as direct as possible. So when do you report? To meet the various requirements you are required to report as soon as the knowledge or suspicion comes to your mind. It means that you may be reporting before the 'transaction' is undertaken, while it is being undertaken, or after completion of the transaction. Let us take the last one first – post-transactional reporting. This has historically been the usual way and timing for the vast majority of reports and there is no doubt that this will continue to be the case. As to how long after the event you can report, there is no time limit. The reason for this is that many transactions are not pre-advised and with the increasing use of e-commerce and similar direct business transactions there is no intervention in many transactions. However, if you are pre-advised of a suspicious transaction you must report it immediately; it is not an option to leave it until after the transaction is completed. So what do you do if you know or suspect before the transaction is undertaken? You must report to NCIS and request consent to continue with the transaction.

CONSENT

The making of event reports does not usually cause immediate problems for the MLRO or the firm. The problem area tends to revolve around the need to report before the transaction is undertaken. We discussed the rule of consent in Chapter 7 but what exactly are the problems involved? The main difficulty is handling your customer relationship if completion of the transaction is delayed while awaiting consent or, more importantly, if consent is refused over the further timescale of 31 days given to the authorities. One of the main problems is to avoid the problem of 'tipping off'. There is no guaranteed best way of handling consent requests. Each case has to be handled on its merits, but co-operation with the authorities is always helpful. NCIS is fully aware of the problems consent delays can lead to, and handles them as quickly as possible. The latest statistics from NCIS show that it handles 88 per cent of consent requests within a day of submission.

LEGAL PRIVILEGE

This is an area of great confusion, doubt and worry for lawyers. Basically, if information comes to a lawyer's notice in 'privileged circumstances' then he has a defence for not reporting, provided it is not done for the committing of a criminal act. The problem is, what are privileged circumstances? It is here that the debate gets confusing. 'Privileged circumstances' certainly seem to cover information or material provided as part of legal proceedings or contemplated proceedings. Other than this, it now appears extremely doubtful whether privileged circumstances exist. From a lawyer's point of view, one of their major concerns involves the ease with which they could breach Section 328 of the Proceeds of Crime Act. This concern revolves around what constitutes an 'arrangement' and the need for them to seek consent before acting, especially in litigation proceedings.

At the time of writing, the most significant case is *Bowman* v. *Fels*, which the Court of Appeal heard in 2005. This case seemed to make it clear that the phrase in Section 328 of 'enters into or becomes concerned in an arrangement' would not normally cover conduct of legal proceedings. Thus it appears that, for litigation matters, lawyers do not have to seek consent. Of course, this would not include what one might describe as 'sham litigation' (that is, litigation created especially for the purpose of money laundering). There is also the question of when does litigation actually start, since the Court of Appeal speaks of it as 'litigation from the issue of proceedings and the securing of injunctive relief or a freezing order up to its final disposal by judgment'. So what happens to anything outside this timescale: is this privileged or not?

While this decision is helpful and will undoubtedly reduce the number of consent requests being made to NCIS, it also leaves many questions unanswered. Prudence is obviously therefore necessary since if lawyers think they have a defence under Bowman but this later proves to be incorrect, then they have committed the criminal act of failing to report and acting without consent. Equally, if they report unnecessarily, would their client have a right of action for breach of confidentiality?

The one thing that is certain is that this decision only involves lawyers and no other profession. It must also be remembered that the basis of this case was the need to seek consent under Section 328 and the decision answers that question and not the need to report under other aspects of the Proceeds of Crime Act, the Terrorism Act or the Money Laundering Regulations.

CHAPTER 15

The Role of the Money Laundering Reporting Officer (MLRO)

As we have seen, the position of the MLRO is fundamental to many aspects of meeting the anti-money laundering requirements. Indeed, within firms regulated by the FSA, this has now become an extremely important role. The position is a 'controlled function' and as such can only be held by an 'approved person'.

We have discussed the MLRO elsewhere in the book (see Chapters 11, 13, 14, 16 and 17) but here we will look at the responsibilities of the job and its background and history. The law requires the appointment of a 'nominated person' to carry out various functions including the receiving of internal suspicion reports. This job, known as the MLRO, became the standard description of the job in many countries. In fact this designation became so commonly used that when the FSA issued its Money Laundering Sourcebook, it used the term for their newly created 'controlled function'. It has now become a formally required position in all regulated businesses. While the MLRO does not have to be the same person as the 'nominated person' required by law, the way the FSA has drawn up the responsibilities of the MLRO, in most firms the two jobs are combined. However, the duties imposed by the FSA are much more onerous than simply dealing with suspicion reports.

So what does the Sourcebook actually say?

- A relevant firm must set up and operate arrangements including the appointment of a money laundering reporting officer.[1]

- The MLRO is responsible for the oversight of the relevant firm's anti-money laundering activities and is the key person in the relevant firm's implementation of anti-money laundering strategies and policies.[2]

---

1   Financial Services Authority Sourcebook – Rule 2.1.1.
2   Financial Services Authority Sourcebook – Guidance 2.1.2.

- The MLRO must act as the focal point within the firm for the oversight of *all* activities relating to anti-money laundering.[3]

How does the FSA expect this to be translated into practice? In other words, what do they consider the duties and responsibilities of an MLRO to be in a regulated firm? To:

- monitor the day-to-day operation of the firm's anti-money laundering policies;

- respond promptly to any reasonable request for information made by the FSA;

- receive internal reports;

- take reasonable steps to access any relevant 'know your business' information;

- make external reports to the NCIS;

- obtain and use national and international findings concerning countries with inadequacies in the approach to money laundering prevention;

- take reasonable steps to establish and maintain adequate arrangements for awareness and training; and

- make compliance reports to the relevant firm's managers at least annually.

It is clear that the FSA considers the MLRO to be the focal point within all regulated firms in respect of all aspects of anti-money laundering policies and procedures. From this it can be seen that the MLRO is now a specialist job and it is now one of the most important positions in any firm within the regulated sector. As has already been said, it is a 'controlled function' and as such must be held by a person who fully complies with the 'approved persons regime'. To be an approved person, what is required, and how must they act in all their professional dealings? The following is necessary:

- Individuals must act with integrity.

- Individuals must act with skill, care and diligence.

- Individuals must observe proper standards of market conduct.

---

3   Financial Services Authority Sourcebook – Guidance 7.1.1.

- Individuals must deal with the FSA in an open and co-operative way.

Who is the best person to undertake such a wide-ranging and important function? What requirements, knowledge and experience are needed for this job? Clearly, to achieve all that is required of them, an MLRO in a regulated firm must be a member of senior management and be able to operate both independently and autonomously. They must possess the trust and confidence of both management and staff of the firm as well as that of the FSA. In addition, they also must warrant the trust and confidence of the enforcement agencies. To satisfactorily undertake the duties they must have sufficient knowledge of the organisation, its products, services and systems. They must have access to all relevant information throughout the organisation and, of course, have knowledge of the existence of such information.

To undertake all these responsibilities, what does the MLRO have to have? Primarily, they need a good understanding of:

- the Money Laundering Regulations;

- the FSA's Money Laundering Sourcebook;

- UK Statutes concerning offences and defences related to money laundering, particularly the Proceeds of Crime Act 2002 and the Terrorism Act 2000;

- international standards relating to money laundering prevention procedures, legislation and regulations worldwide;

- typologies of money laundering and the financial sector's vulnerability by both product and service;

- the MLRO's own firm including its products, processes and key personnel and their various vulnerabilities to money laundering;

- what constitutes a suspicious transaction, bearing in mind the 'objective test' and when and how to make a report. Also when and how to seek 'consent' from NCIS to undertake a transaction;

- how investigations are carried out, how evidence is collected and the obligations imposed by the various court orders which can be served on the institution; and

- the organisation and key personnel of the National Criminal Intelligence Service, Serious Organised Crime Agency, FSA, police and HM Revenue and Customs.

CHAPTER 16

The Money Laundering Reporting Officer's Annual Report

The requirements for the production of what is generally referred to as the MLRO's Report are laid down in the FSA Sourcebook. This report is considered to be a fundamental part of a firm's compliance monitoring. While the requirement for this report is covered in the FSA Money Laundering Sourcebook under ML 7.2, it forms a fundamental part of the firm's overall compliance obligations. Indeed, it is linked directly to the Senior Management Arrangements, Systems and Controls (SYSC) section of the FSA Handbook which covers the responsibilities placed upon a firm's senior management for its overall management and control. However, although the production of this report is only a regulatory requirement for firms regulated by the FSA, the concept is valid for any business, particularly medium to large ones.

Let us first look at what the FSA actually requires.

ML 7.2 Compliance monitoring[1]

ML 7.2.1 SYSC 3.2.6 R (Compliance[2]) requires a relevant firm to take reasonable care to establish and maintain appropriate systems and controls for compliance with its regulatory obligations and to counter the risk that it might be used to further financial crime. This section amplifies particular aspects of the rule in SYSC. It does not, however, limit the application of the rule, the effect of which is that, where financial crime is concerned, firms must also comply with other Handbook requirements (in particular, ML) and their legal obligations under the Money Laundering Regulations and the Proceeds of Crime Act 2002.

ML 7.2.2 (1) A relevant firm should establish and maintain arrangements under SYSC 3.2.6 R which include requirements that:

---

1   Financial Services Authority Sourcebook ML 7.2.
2   SYSC 3.2.6 R: A firm must take reasonable care to establish and maintain effective systems and controls for compliance with applicable requirements and standards under the regulatory system and for countering the risk that the firm might be used to further financial crime.

(a)   at least once in each calendar year, the relevant firm
         commission a report from its MLRO which:

   (i)   assesses the relevant firm's compliance with this
            sourcebook;

   (ii)   indicates, in particular, the way in which new findings
            under ML 5 (Using national and international findings)
            have been used during the year; and

   (iii)   gives the number of reports made in accordance with
            ML 4.1 (Internal reporting) by staff of the relevant firm,
            dealing separately, if appropriate, with different parts of
            the relevant firm's business;

(b)   the relevant firm's senior management consider the report;
         and

(c)   they take any necessary action to remedy deficiencies identified
         by the report.

(2) Contravention of (1) may be relied on as tending to establish
contravention of SYSC 3.2.6 R.

ML 7.2.3 Figures for internal reports should be broken down, if
appropriate, in the MLRO's report. The purpose of the report is to enable
a relevant firm's senior management to assess whether internal reports
are being made whenever required by ML 4.1.2 R, and that an overall
figure which seems satisfactory does not conceal inadequate reporting
in a particular part of the relevant firm's business. Relevant firms will
need to use their judgement how the MLRO should be required to break
down the figures in order to achieve this aim.

When reading the above, the first thing that strikes you is that it is not for
the MLRO to make a report to senior management but it is the responsibility
of senior management to 'commission a report' from the MLRO. This is an
important difference and one that is frequently not appreciated. By wording
the requirement in this way the FSA is placing responsibility for ensuring
adequate compliance where it rightly belongs: on the shoulders of senior
management. The other thing that one must observe is that this report must be
commissioned 'at least once a year'. That means, therefore, that it does not have
to be an 'annual report'; it can be required more frequently, and there may be
many circumstances when this is necessary.

The use of this important report, if it is properly and fully produced, can help a number of different people. From senior management's point of view, this report provides them with a detailed summary of the institution's compliance with anti-money laundering regulations. It should highlight not only those areas where the firm is complying, but all areas where there are shortcomings or a need for improvement. The report obviously must cover all aspects and any problems or deficiencies in KYC, KYB, monitoring procedures and the reporting to NCIS including statistics, record-keeping and staff training. It should also be used to advise senior management of any proposed changes in either legislation or regulations, or proposals put forward by the FSA. Senior management should also be kept aware of both national and international findings.

A careful examination of this report will enable senior management to ascertain what actions need to be taken and where. Of course, there may be a downside to all this since now that senior management know all the deficiencies and problems in the firm, then clearly they will have to take action to correct them, otherwise they could be found culpable by the FSA under their overall Systems and Management responsibilities.

If the MLRO's report highlights significant failings or shortcomings, senior management must devise and implement a process of correction. This is where it may be necessary to seek a further report, or report over the course of the following year. If there are significant changes or improvements necessary, no responsible senior management would want to wait until the next 'annual report' to see if they had been introduced and were effective.

The second party who can benefit from the MLRO's Report is the MLRO. It has been described by some as the MLRO's safety valve. It is the one place where the MLRO can formally detail and bring to the attention of senior management any problems they have in carrying out their important function. Classic examples are insufficient resources or lack of co-operation from staff, particularly management. Here, again, it will put the onus on senior management to take the necessary action. It will also be a form of 'safeguard' for the MLRO, whereby they can demonstrate to the FSA, or other authorities, that they have made senior management aware of all the firm's deficiencies and problems, together with any reasons why the MLRO has been unable to fully comply with their responsibilities.

The third and final party which benefits from these reports is the FSA itself. The report not only enables it to monitor a firm's compliance with the regulations but also highlights any problems or difficulties it has. It also enables the FSA to gauge the response by senior management to their firm's problems and the actions they take to correct any deficiencies.

CHAPTER 17

Awareness and Training

This has now become one of the most important aspects of the fight against money laundering. It is covered both in the Proceeds of Crime Act, the Money Laundering Regulations and in the Financial Services Authorities Sourcebook.

Section 330 (7)(b) of the Proceeds of Crime Act actually provides an employee with a defence for failing to report if they have not been provided by their employers with adequate training. Such a defence, if successfully used, would leave the employer in a difficult position in view of the requirements of the Money Laundering Regulations.

So what do the Money Laundering Regulations 2003 require? Regulation 3 requires that each regulated institution takes reasonable measures to make its employees aware of its policies, procedures and the various enactments and regulations relating to money laundering. This training must include how to recognise and deal with transactions which may be related to money laundering as well as the tipping-off provisions. It must also provide relevant employees with appropriate training from time to time. This is a requirement imposed upon all persons or firms which are covered by or fall within the terms of the Money Laundering Regulations' requirements.

The legal position seems clear; but the requirements of the FSA are even more precise and detailed. This subject is covered in Chapter 6 of the FSA Sourcebook which imposes on all firms the obligation to provide effective awareness or training, in order to ensure that employees in the relevant institutions provide both awareness and training.

AWARENESS

FSA Rule 6.2.1 and the Regulations require that an institution must take the necessary steps to ensure that employees who handle, or are managerially responsible for the handling of, transactions which may involve money laundering are aware of:

- their responsibilities under the Sourcebook including those for obtaining sufficient evidence of identity, recognising and reporting knowledge or suspicion of money laundering, and the use of findings of material deficiencies;

- the identity and the responsibilities of the MLRO;

- the law relating to money laundering, including the Money Laundering Regulations 2003 and the Sourcebook; and

- the potential effect of money laundering on the institution, on its employees and its clients, of any breach of the law.

TRAINING

The FSA considers training to be separate from awareness, and provides for it under Rule 6.3.1. Under this Rule, the FSA requires the institution to take reasonable steps to provide appropriate anti-money laundering training for its employees who handle, or are managerially responsible for the handling of, transactions which may involve money laundering. This Rule is supported by Evidential Provision 6.3.2 which indicates that the institution should provide training which:

(a)   *deals with the law on money laundering, and the respon-sibilities of staff under the institution's arrangements;*

(b)   *is applicable to all staff who handle or are managerially responsible for the handling of transactions which may involve money laundering;*

(c)   *takes place with sufficient frequency to ensure that within any period of 24 months it is given to substantially all relevant staff.*

As can be seen, the FSA's requirements far exceed the basics required by the law and are far more comprehensive. Its requirements are such that any firm which fails to implement them will be in breach of the FSA Rules and will thus be liable to severe regulatory sanction. The Sourcebook goes further, in that it states that it is the MLRO's specific responsibility to ensure that awareness and training requirements are met. Although technically the MLRO has the responsibility for this, it is accepted and recognised that they cannot undertake this work personally. It can be provided by other areas of the firm or outsourced but, no matter how it is provided, the responsibility remains with the MLRO. Also, the timing cannot be set in stone. While everyone must receive refresher training at least every two years, certain positions and functions may require a more frequent training/awareness regime. This is really another aspect of a risk-based approach and MLROs must use their judgement to fix the training programme schedule. It does not matter about the timing fixed in the schedule; the MLRO must always be aware of any new staff or staff who change their duties, to ensure that they receive the necessary training for their new position.

No matter how awareness or training is provided or by whom, it is essential that proper records are kept. These records must show who has been trained and when, what training was provided and some means of ensuring that they understood the training. This latter aspect is also vital, as you have to be able to demonstrate that all staff have understood the training so that they understand both their own personal responsibilities and those of their employer. It must never be forgotten that staff members have a personal legal responsibility under the anti-money laundering legislation. If they fail to act properly, then they can face a personal criminal charge which could result in a long period of imprisonment. It behoves an employer, whether or not there is a regulatory requirement, to ensure that all its employees are aware of their personal legal risk.

To ensure that this is being done and in order for you to demonstrate the fact that you have met both the legal requirements and the FSA requirements, if appropriate, it is essential that full detailed records of all staff awareness and training are kept.

Relevant Business[1]

For the purposes of these Regulations, 'relevant business' means:

    (a)   the regulated activity of:

        (i)   accepting deposits;

        (ii)   effecting or carrying out contracts of long-term insurance when carried on by a person who has received official authorisation pursuant to Article 4 or 51 of the Life Assurance Consolidation Directive;

        (iii)   dealing in investments as principal or as agent;

        (iv)   arranging deals in investments;

        (v)   managing investments;

        (vi)   safeguarding and administering investments;

        (vii)   sending dematerialised instructions;

        (viii)   establishing (and taking other steps in relation to) collective investment schemes;

        (ix)   advising on investments; or

        (x)   issuing electronic money;

    (b)   the activities of the National Savings Bank;

    (c)   any activity carried on for the purpose of raising money authorised to be raised under the National Loans Act 1968 under the auspices of the Director of Savings;

    (d)   the business of operating a bureau de change, transmitting money (or any representation of monetary value) by any means or cashing cheques which are made payable to customers;

    (e)   any of the activities in points 1 to 12 or 14 of Annex 1 to the Banking Consolidation Directive (which activities are, for convenience, set out in Schedule 1 to these Regulations)

---

1   Money Laundering Regulations 2003 – Regulation 2(2).

when carried on by way of business, ignoring an activity falling within any of sub-paragraphs (a) to (d);

(f)   *estate agency work;*

(g)   *operating a casino by way of business;*

(h)   *the activities of a person appointed to act as an insolvency practitioner within the meaning of Section 388 of the Insolvency Act 1986 or Article 3 of the Insolvency (Northern Ireland) Order 1989;*

(i)   *the provision by way of business of advice about the tax affairs of another person by a body corporate or unincorporated or, in the case of a sole practitioner, by an individual;*

(j)   *the provision by way of business of accountancy services by a body corporate or unincorporated or, in the case of a sole practitioner, by an individual;*

(k)   *the provision by way of business of audit services by a person who is eligible for appointment as a company auditor under Section 25 of the Companies Act 1989 or Article 28 of the Companies (Northern Ireland) Order 1990;*

(l)   *the provision by way of business of legal services by a body corporate or unincorporated or, in the case of a sole practitioner, by an individual and which involves participation in a financial or real property transaction (whether by assisting in the planning or execution of any such transaction or otherwise by acting for, or on behalf of, a client in any such transaction);*

(m)   *the provision by way of business of services in relation to the formation, operation or management of a company or a trust; or*

(n)   *the activity of dealing in goods of any description by way of business (including dealing as an auctioneer) whenever a transaction involves accepting a total cash payment of 15,000 euro or more.*

SCHEDULE 1[2]

ACTIVITIES LISTED IN ANNEX 1 TO THE BANKING CONSOLIDATION DIRECTIVE

1. *Acceptance of deposits and other repayable funds.*

2. *Lending.*

3. *Financial leasing.*

4. *Money transmission services.*

5. *Issuing and administrating means of payment (e.g., credit cards, travellers' cheques and bankers' drafts).*

6. *Guarantees and commitments.*

7. *Trading for own account or for account of customers in:*

    (a)   *money market instruments (cheques, bills, certificates of deposit, etc.);*

    (b)   *foreign exchange;*

    (c)   *financial futures and options;*

    (d)   *exchange and interest-rate instruments;*

    (e)   *transferable securities.*

8. *Participation in securities issues and the provision of services related to such issues.*

9. *Advice to undertakings on capital structure, industrial strategy and related questions and advice as well as services relating to mergers and purchase of undertakings.*

10. *Money broking.*

11. *Portfolio management and advice.*

12. *Safekeeping and administration of securities.*

13. *Credit reference services.*

14. *Safe custody services.*

---

2   Money Laundering Regulations 2003 – Schedule 1.

Regulation 5[1]

(1) Except in circumstances falling within regulation 4(2)(b)(i), identification procedures under regulation 4 do not require A to take steps to obtain evidence of any person's identity in any of the following circumstances.

(2) Where A has reasonable grounds for believing that B:

    (a) carries on in the United Kingdom relevant business falling within any of the sub-paragraphs (a) to (e) of regulation 2(2), is not a money service operator and, if carrying on an activity falling within regulation 2(2)(a), is an authorised person with permission under the 2000 Act[2] to carry on that activity;

    (b) does not carry on relevant business in the United Kingdom but does carry on comparable activities to those falling within sub-paragraph (a) and is covered by the Money Laundering Directive; or

    (c) is regulated by an overseas regulatory authority (within the meaning given by section 82 of the Companies Act 1989) and is based or incorporated in a country (other than a European Economic Area (EEA) State) whose law contains comparable provisions to those contained in the Money Laundering Directive.

(3) Where:

    (a) A carries out a one-off transaction with or for a third party pursuant to an introduction effected by a person who has provided a written assurance that evidence of the identity of all third parties introduced by him will have been obtained and recorded under procedures maintained by him;

    (b) that person identifies the third party; and

    (c) A has reasonable grounds for believing that that person falls within any of sub-paragraphs (a) to (c) of paragraph (2).

---

1   Money Laundering Regulations 2003 – Regulation 5.
2   '2000 Act' means the Financial Services and Markets Act 2000.

(4) In relation to a contract of long-term insurance:

    (a)   *in connection with a pension scheme taken out by virtue of a person's contract of employment or occupation where the contract of long-term insurance:*

        (i)   *contains no surrender clause; and*

        (ii)   *may not be used as collateral for a loan; or*

    (b)   *in respect of which a premium is payable:*

        (i)   *in one instalment of an amount not exceeding 2500 euro; or*

        (ii)   *periodically and where the total payable in respect of any calendar year does not exceed 1000 euro.*

(5) Where the proceeds of a one-off transaction are payable to B but are instead directly reinvested on his behalf in another transaction:

    (a)   *of which a record is kept; and*

    (b)   *which can result only in another reinvestment made on B's behalf or in a payment made directly to B.*

Meaning of Customer Information[1]

(1) 'Customer Information', in relation to a person and a financial institution, is information on whether the person holds, or has held, an account or accounts at the financial institution (whether solely or jointly with another) and (if so) information as to:

(a) the matters specified in subsection (2) if the person is an individual;

(b) the matters specified in subsection (3) if the person is a company or limited liability partnership or a similar body incorporated or otherwise established outside the United Kingdom.

(2) The matters referred to in subsection (1)(a) are:

(a) the account number or numbers;

(b) the person's full name;

(c) his date of birth;

(d) his most recent address and any previous addresses;

(e) the date or dates on which he began to hold the account or accounts and, if he has ceased to hold the account or any of the accounts, the date or dates on which he did so;

(f) such evidence of his identity as was obtained by the financial institution under or for the purposes of any legislation relating to money laundering;

(g) the full name, date of birth and most recent address, and any previous addresses, of any person who holds, or has held, an account at the financial institution jointly with him;

(h) the account number or numbers of any other account or accounts held at the financial institution to which he is a

---

1 Proceeds of Crime Act 2002, Section 364 as amended by the Serious Organised Crime and Police Act 2005.

*signatory, and details of the person holding the other account
or accounts.*

(3) The matters referred to in subsection (1)(b) are:

(a)   *the account number or numbers;*

(b)   *the person's full name;*

(c)   *a description of any business which the person carries on;*

(d)   *the country or territory in which it is incorporated or
otherwise established and any number allocated to it under
the Companies Act 1985 (c.6) or corresponding legislation of
any country or territory outside the United Kingdom;*

(e)   *any number assigned to it for the purposes of value added tax
in the United Kingdom;*

(f)   *its registered office, and any previous registered offices, under
the Companies Act 1985 or the Companies (Northern Ireland)
Order 1986 (S.I. 1986/1032 (N.I. 6)) or anything similar
under corresponding legislation of any country or territory
outside the United Kingdom;*

(g)   *its registered office, and any previous registered offices,
under the Limited Liability Partnerships Act 2000 (c.12)
or anything similar under corresponding legislation of any
country or territory outside Great Britain;*

(h)   *the date or dates on which it began to hold the account or
accounts and, if it has ceased to hold the account or any of the
accounts, the date or dates on which it did so;*

(i)   *such evidence of its identity as was obtained by the financial
institution under or for the purposes of any legislation
relating to money laundering;*

(j)   *the full name, date of birth and most recent address
and any previous addresses of any person who is
a signatory to the account or any of the accounts.*

*(4) The Secretary of State may by order provide for information of a
description specified in the order:*

(a)   *to be customer information, or*

    (b)   *no longer to be customer information.*

(5) Money laundering is an act which:

    (a)   *constitutes an offence under Section 327, 328 or 329 of this Act or Section 18 of the Terrorism Act 2000 (c.11), or*

    (aa)   *constitutes an offence specified in Section 415(1A) of this Act; or*

    (b)   *would constitute an offence specified in paragraph (a) or (aa) if done in the United Kingdom.*

Terrorism Act 2000 as amended by the Anti-terrorism, Crime and Security Act 2001

15 – (1) A person commits an offence if he:

    (a)   invites another to provide money or other property, and

    (b)   intends that it should be used, or has reasonable cause to suspect that it may be used, for the purposes of terrorism.

  (2) A person commits an offence if he:

    (a)   receives money or other property, and

    (b)   intends that it should be used, or has reasonable cause to suspect that it may be used, for the purposes of terrorism.

  (3) A person commits an offence if he:

    (a)   provides money or other property, and

    (b)   knows or has reasonable cause to suspect that it will or may be used for the purposes of terrorism.

    (a)   (4) In this section a reference to the provision of money or other property is a reference to its being given, lent or otherwise made available, whether or not for consideration.

16 – (1) A person commits an offence if he uses money or other property for the purposes of terrorism.

  (2) A person commits an offence if he:

    (a)   possesses money or other property, and

    (b)   intends that it should be used, or has reasonable cause to suspect that it may be used, for the purposes of terrorism.

17 – A person commits an offence if:

(a)   *he enters into or becomes concerned in an arrangement as a result of which money or other property is made available or is to be made available to another, and*

(b)   *he knows or has reasonable cause to suspect that it will or may be used for the purposes of terrorism.*

18 – (1) A person commits an offence if he enters into or becomes concerned in an arrangement which facilitates the retention or control by or on behalf of another person of terrorist property:

(a)   *by concealment,*

(b)   *by removal from the jurisdiction,*

(c)   *by transfer to nominees, or*

(d)   *in any way.*

(2) It is a defence for a person charged with an offence under subsection (1) to prove that he did not know and had no reasonable cause to suspect that the arrangement related to terrorist property.

19 – (1) This section applies where a person:

(a)   *believes or suspects that another person has committed an offence under any of Sections 15 to 18, and*

(b)   *bases his belief or suspicion on information which comes to his attention in the course of a trade, profession, business or employment.*

(2) The person commits an offence if he does not disclose to a constable as soon as is reasonably practicable:

(a)   *his belief or suspicion, and*

(b)   *the information on which it is based.*

(3) It is a defence for a person charged with an offence under subsection (2) to prove that he had a reasonable excuse for not making the disclosure.

(4) Where:

(a)   *a person is in employment,*

(b)   *his employer has established a procedure for the making of disclosures of the matters specified in subsection (2), and*

(c)   *he is charged with an offence under that subsection, it is a defence for him to prove that he disclosed the matters specified in that subsection in accordance with the procedure.*

(5) Subsection (2) does not require disclosure by a professional legal adviser of:

(a)   *information which he obtains in privileged circumstances, or*

(b)   *a belief or suspicion based on information which he obtains in privileged circumstances.*

(6) For the purpose of subsection (5), information is obtained by an adviser in privileged circumstances if it comes to him, otherwise than with a view to furthering a criminal purpose:

(a)   *from a client or a client's representative, in connection with the provision of legal advice by the adviser to the client,*

(b)   *from a person seeking legal advice from the adviser, or from the person's representative, or*

(c)   *from any person, for the purpose of actual or contemplated legal proceedings.*

(7) For the purposes of subsection (1)(a) a person shall be treated as having committed an offence under one of Sections 15 to 18 if:

(a)   *he has taken an action or been in possession of a thing, and*

(b)   *he would have committed an offence under one of these sections if he had been in the United Kingdom at the time when he took the action or was in possession of the thing.*

(8) A person guilty of a offence under this section shall be liable:

(a)   *on conviction on indictment, to imprisonment for a term not exceeding five years, to a fine or to both, or*

(b)   *on summary conviction, to imprisonment for a term not exceeding six months, or to a fine not exceeding the statutory maximum or to both.*

20 – (1) A person may disclose to a constable:

    (a)   a suspicion or belief that any moneys, or other property, is terrorist property or is derived from terrorist property;

    (b)   any matter on which the suspicion or belief is based.

(2) A person may make a disclosure to a constable in the circumstances mentioned in Sections 19(1) and (2).

(3) Subsections (1) and (2) shall have effect notwithstanding any restriction on the disclosure of information imposed by statute or otherwise.

(4) Where:

    (a)   a person is in employment, and

    (b)   his employer has established a procedure for the making of disclosures of the kinds mentioned in subsection (1) and section 19(2), subsections (1) and (2) shall have effect in relation to that person as if any reference to disclosure to a constable included a reference to disclosure in accordance with the procedure.

21 – (1) A person does not commit an offence under any of Sections 15 to 18 if he is acting with the express consent of a constable.

(2) Subject to subsections (3) and (4), a person does not commit an offence under any of Sections 15 to 18 by involvement in a transaction or arrangement relating to money or other property if he discloses to a constable:

    (a)   his suspicions or belief that the money or other property is terrorist property, and

    (b)   the information on which his suspicion or belief is based.

(3) Subsection (2) applies only where a person makes a disclosure:

    (a)   after he becomes concerned in the transaction concerned,

    (b)   on his own initiative, and

    (c)   as soon as is reasonably practical.

(4) Subsection (2) does not apply to a person if:

(a)   *a constable forbids him to continue his involvement in the transaction or arrangement to which the disclosure relates, and*

(b)   *he continues his involvement.*

(5) It is a defence for a person charged with an offence under any of Sections 15(2) and 15(3) and 16 to 18 to prove that:

(a)   *he intended to make a disclosure of the kind mentioned in subsections (2) and (3), and*

(b)   *there is a reasonable excuse for his failure to do so.*

(6) Where:

(a)   *a person is in employment, and*

(b)   *his employer has established a procedure for the making of disclosures of the same kind as may be made to a constable under subsection (2), this subsection shall have effect in relation to that person as if any reference to disclosure to a constable included a reference to disclosure in accordance with the procedures.*

(7) A reference in this section to a transaction or arrangement relating to money or other property includes a reference to use or possession.

21A – 'Failure to disclose': regulated sector:

(1) A person commits an offence if each of the following three conditions is satisfied.

(2) The first condition is that he:

(a)   *knows or suspects, or*

(b)   *has reasonable grounds for knowing or suspecting, that another person has committed an offence under any of Sections 15 to 18.*

(3) The second condition is that the information or other matter:

(a)   *on which his knowledge or suspicion is based, or*

(b)   *which gives reasonable grounds for such knowledge or suspicion, came to him in the course of a business in the regulated sector.*

(4) The third condition is that he does not disclose the information or other matter to a constable or a nominated officer as soon as is practicable after it comes to him.

(5) But a person does not commit an offence under this section if:

  (a)   he has reasonable excuse for not disclosing the information or other matter,

  (b)   he is a professional legal adviser and the information or other matter came to him in privileged circumstances.

(6) In deciding whether a person committed an offence under this section, the court must consider whether he followed any relevant guidance which was at the time concerned:

  (a)   issued by a supervisory authority or any other appropriate body,

  (b)   approved by the Treasury, and

  (c)   published in a manner it approved as appropriate in its opinion to bring the guidance to the attention of persons likely to be affected by it.

(7) A disclosure to a nominated officer is a disclosure which:

  (a)   is made to a person nominated by the alleged offender's employer to receive disclosures under this section, and

  (b)   is made in the course of the alleged offender's employment and in accordance with the procedure established by the employer for the purpose.

(8) Information or other matter comes to a professional legal adviser in privileged circumstances if it is communicated or given to him:

  (a)   by (or by a representative of) a client of his in connection with the giving by the adviser of legal advice to the client,

  (b)   by (or by a representative of) a person seeking legal advice from the adviser, or

  (c)   by a person in connection with legal proceedings or contemplated legal proceedings.

(9) But subsection (8) does not apply to information or other matter which is communicated or given with a view to furthering a criminal purpose.

(10) Schedule 3A has effect for the purpose of determining what is:

    (a)   a business in the regulated sector,

    (b)   a supervisory authority.

(11) For the purpose of subsection (2), a person is to be taken to have committed an offence there mentioned if:

    (a)   he has taken an action or been in possession of a thing, and

    (b)   he would have committed the offence if he had been in the United Kingdom at the time when he took the action or was in possession of the thing.

(12) A person guilty of an offence under this section is liable:

    (a)   on conviction on indictment, to imprisonment for a term not exceeding five years or a fine or to both;

    (b)   on summary conviction, to imprisonment for a term not exceeding six months or to a fine not exceeding the statutory maximum or to both.

(13) An appropriate body is any body which regulates or is representative of any trade, profession, business or employment carried on by the alleged offender.

(14) The reference to a constable includes a reference to a person authorised for the purpose of this section by the Director-General of the National Criminal Intelligence Service.

The Forty Recommendations

Financial Action Task Force on Money Laundering/ Group d'action financière sur le blanchiment de capitaux (FATF/GAFI)

INTRODUCTION

Money laundering methods and techniques change in response to developing counter-measures. In recent years, the Financial Action Task Force (FATF)[1] has noted increasingly sophisticated combinations of techniques, such as the increased use of legal persons to disguise the true ownership and control of illegal proceeds, and an increased use of professionals to provide advice and assistance in laundering criminal funds. These factors, combined with the experience gained through the FATF's Non-Cooperative Countries and Territories process, and a number of national and international initiatives, led the FATF to review and revise the Forty Recommendations into a new comprehensive framework for combating money laundering and terrorist financing. The FATF now calls upon all countries to take the necessary steps to bring their national systems for combating money laundering and terrorist financing into compliance with the new FATF Recommendations, and to effectively implement these measures.

The review process for revising the Forty Recommendations was an extensive one, open to FATF members, non-members, observers, financial and other affected sectors and interested parties. This consultation process provided a wide range of input, all of which was considered in the review process.

The revised Forty Recommendations now apply not only to money laundering but also to terrorist financing, and when combined with the Eight Special Recommendations on Terrorist Financing provide an enhanced, comprehensive and consistent framework of measures for combating money

---

1   The FATF is an inter-governmental body which sets standards, and develops and promotes policies to combat money laundering and terrorist financing. It currently has 33 members: 31 countries and governments and two international organisations; and more than 20 observers: five FATF-style regional bodies and more than 15 other international organisations or bodies. A list of all members and observers can be found on the FATF website at http://www.fatf-gafi. org/Members_en.htm.

laundering and terrorist financing. The FATF recognises that countries have diverse legal and financial systems and so all cannot take identical measures to achieve the common objective, especially over matters of detail. The Recommendations therefore set minimum standards for action for countries to implement the detail according to their particular circumstances and constitutional frameworks. The Recommendations cover all the measures that national systems should have in place within their criminal justice and regulatory systems; the preventive measures to be taken by financial institutions and certain other businesses and professions; and international co-operation.

The original FATF Forty Recommendations were drawn up in 1990 as an initiative to combat the misuse of financial systems by persons laundering drug money. In 1996 the Recommendations were revised for the first time to reflect evolving money laundering typologies. The 1996 Forty Recommendations have been endorsed by more than 130 countries and are the international anti-money laundering standard.

In October 2001 the FATF expanded its mandate to deal with the issue of the financing of terrorism, and took the important step of creating the Eight Special Recommendations on Terrorist Financing. These Recommendations contain a set of measures aimed at combating the funding of terrorist acts and terrorist organisations, and are complementary to the Forty Recommendations.[2]

A key element in the fight against money laundering and the financing of terrorism is the need for countries' systems to be monitored and evaluated, with respect to these international standards. The mutual evaluations conducted by the FATF and FATF-style regional bodies, as well as the assessments conducted by the IMF and World Bank, are a vital mechanism for ensuring that the FATF Recommendations are effectively implemented by all countries.

---

2   The FATF Forty and Eight Special Recommendations have been recognised by the International Monetary Fund and the World Bank as the international standards for combating money laundering and the financing of terrorism.

THE FORTY RECOMMENDATIONS

A. LEGAL SYSTEMS

Scope of the criminal offence of money laundering

1. Countries should criminalise money laundering on the basis of the United Nations Convention against Illicit Traffic in Narcotic Drugs and Psychotropic Substances, 1988 (the Vienna Convention) and the United Nations Convention against Transnational Organized Crime, 2000 (the Palermo Convention).

Countries should apply the crime of money laundering to all serious offences, with a view to including the widest range of predicate offences. Predicate offences may be described by reference to all offences, or to a threshold linked either to a category of serious offences or to the penalty of imprisonment applicable to the predicate offence (threshold approach), or to a list of predicate offences, or a combination of these approaches.

Where countries apply a threshold approach, predicate offences should at a minimum comprise all offences that fall within the category of serious offences under their national law or should include offences which are punishable by a maximum penalty of more than one year's imprisonment, or for those countries that have a minimum threshold for offences in their legal system, predicate offences should comprise all offences, which are punished by a minimum penalty of more than six months' imprisonment.

Whichever approach is adopted, each country should at a minimum include a range of offences within each of the designated categories of offences.[3]

Predicate offences for money laundering should extend to conduct that occurred in another country, which constitutes an offence in that country, and which would have constituted a predicate offence had it occurred domestically. Countries may provide that the only prerequisite is that the conduct would have constituted a predicate offence had it occurred domestically.

Countries may provide that the offence of money laundering does not apply to persons who committed the predicate offence, where this is required by fundamental principles of their domestic law.

2. Countries should ensure that:

---

3   See the definition of 'designated categories of offences' in the Glossary.

a) The intent and knowledge required to prove the offence of money laundering is consistent with the standards set forth in the Vienna and Palermo Conventions, including the concept that such mental state may be inferred from objective factual circumstances.

b) Criminal liability, and, where that is not possible, civil or administrative liability, should apply to legal persons. This should not preclude parallel criminal, civil or administrative proceedings with respect to legal persons in countries in which such forms of liability are available. Legal persons should be subject to effective, proportionate and dissuasive sanctions. Such measures should be without prejudice to the criminal liability of individuals.

Provisional measures and confiscation

3. Countries should adopt measures similar to those set forth in the Vienna and Palermo Conventions, including legislative measures, to enable their competent authorities to confiscate property laundered, proceeds from money laundering or predicate offences, instrumentalities used in or intended for use in the commission of these offences, or property of corresponding value, without prejudicing the rights of bona fide third parties.

Such measures should include the authority to: (a) identify, trace and evaluate property which is subject to confiscation; (b) carry out provisional measures, such as freezing and seizing, to prevent any dealing, transfer or disposal of such property; (c) take steps that will prevent or void actions that prejudice the State's ability to recover property that is subject to confiscation; and (d) take any appropriate investigative measures.

Countries may consider adopting measures that allow such proceeds or instrumentalities to be confiscated without requiring a criminal conviction, or which require an offender to demonstrate the lawful origin of the property alleged to be liable to confiscation, to the extent that such a requirement is consistent with the principles of their domestic law.

B. MEASURES TO BE TAKEN BY FINANCIAL INSTITUTIONS AND NON-FINANCIAL BUSINESSES AND PROFESSIONS TO PREVENT MONEY LAUNDERING AND TERRORIST FINANCING

4. Countries should ensure that financial institution secrecy laws do not inhibit implementation of the FATF Recommendations.

Customer due diligence and record-keeping

5.* Financial institutions should not keep anonymous accounts or accounts in obviously fictitious names.

Financial institutions should undertake customer due diligence measures, including identifying and verifying the identity of their customers, when:

- establishing business relations;

- carrying out occasional transactions: (i) above the applicable designated threshold; or (ii) that are wire transfers in the circumstances covered by the Interpretative Note to Special Recommendation VII;

- there is a suspicion of money laundering or terrorist financing; or

- the financial institution has doubts about the veracity or adequacy of previously obtained customer identification data.

The customer due diligence (CDD) measures to be taken are as follows:

a) Identifying the customer and verifying that customer's identity using reliable, independent source documents, data or information.[4]

b) Identifying the beneficial owner, and taking reasonable measures to verify the identity of the beneficial owner such that the financial institution is satisfied that it knows who the beneficial owner is. For legal persons and arrangements this should include financial institutions taking reasonable measures to understand the ownership and control structure of the customer.

c) Obtaining information on the purpose and intended nature of the business relationship.

d) Conducting ongoing due diligence on the business relationship and scrutiny of transactions undertaken throughout the course of that relationship to ensure that the transactions being conducted are consistent with the institution's knowledge of the customer, their business and risk profile, including, where necessary, the source of funds.

---

* Recommendations marked with an asterisk should be read in conjunction with their Interpretative Note.

4 Reliable, independent source documents, data or information will hereafter be referred to as 'identification data'.

Financial institutions should apply each of the CDD measures under (a) to (d) above, but may determine the extent of such measures on a risk-sensitive basis depending on the type of customer, business relationship or transaction. The measures that are taken should be consistent with any guidelines issued by competent authorities. For higher risk categories, financial institutions should perform enhanced due diligence. In certain circumstances, where there are low risks, countries may decide that financial institutions can apply reduced or simplified measures.

Financial institutions should verify the identity of the customer and beneficial owner before or during the course of establishing a business relationship or conducting transactions for occasional customers. Countries may permit financial institutions to complete the verification as soon as reasonably practicable following the establishment of the relationship, where the money laundering risks are effectively managed and where this is essential not to interrupt the normal conduct of business.

Where the financial institution is unable to comply with paragraphs (a) to (c) above, it should not open the account, commence business relations or perform the transaction; or should terminate the business relationship; and should consider making a suspicious transactions report in relation to the customer.

These requirements should apply to all new customers, though financial institutions should also apply this Recommendation to existing customers on the basis of materiality and risk, and should conduct due diligence on such existing relationships at appropriate times.

6. Financial institutions should, in relation to politically exposed persons, in addition to performing normal due diligence measures:

a)   Have appropriate risk management systems to determine whether the customer is a politically exposed person.

b)   Obtain senior management approval for establishing business relationships with such customers.

c)   Take reasonable measures to establish the source of wealth and source of funds.

d)   Conduct enhanced ongoing monitoring of the business relationship.

7. Financial institutions should, in relation to cross-border correspondent banking and other similar relationships, in addition to performing normal due diligence measures:

a)   Gather sufficient information about a respondent institution to understand fully the nature of the respondent's business and to determine from publicly available information the reputation of the institution and the quality of supervision, including whether it has been subject to a money laundering or terrorist financing investigation or regulatory action.

b)   Assess the respondent institution's anti-money laundering and terrorist financing controls.

c)   Obtain approval from senior management before establishing new correspondent relationships.

d)   Document the respective responsibilities of each institution.

e)   With respect to 'payable-through accounts', be satisfied that the respondent bank has verified the identity of and performed ongoing due diligence on the customers having direct access to accounts of the correspondent and that it is able to provide relevant customer identification data upon request to the correspondent bank.

8. Financial institutions should pay special attention to any money laundering threats that may arise from new or developing technologies that might favour anonymity, and take measures, if needed, to prevent their use in money laundering schemes. In particular, financial institutions should have policies and procedures in place to address any specific risks associated with non-face-to-face business relationships or transactions.

9.* Countries may permit financial institutions to rely on intermediaries or other third parties to perform elements (a) – (c) of the CDD process or to introduce business, provided that the criteria set out below are met. Where such reliance is permitted, the ultimate responsibility for customer identification and verification remains with the financial institution relying on the third party.

The criteria that should be met are as follows:

a)   A financial institution relying upon a third party should immediately obtain the necessary information concerning elements (a) – (c) of the CDD process. Financial institutions should take adequate steps to satisfy themselves that copies of identification data and other relevant documentation relating to the CDD requirements will be made available from the third party upon request without delay.

b) The financial institution should satisfy itself that the third party is regulated and supervised for, and has measures in place to comply with CDD requirements in line with Recommendations 5 and 10.

It is left to each country to determine in which countries the third party that meets the conditions can be based, having regard to information available on countries that do not or do not adequately apply the FATF Recommendations.

10.* Financial institutions should maintain, for at least five years, all necessary records on transactions, both domestic or international, to enable them to comply swiftly with information requests from the competent authorities. Such records must be sufficient to permit reconstruction of individual transactions (including the amounts and types of currency involved if any) so as to provide, if necessary, evidence for prosecution of criminal activity.

Financial institutions should keep records on the identification data obtained through the customer due diligence process (for example, copies or records of official identification documents like passports, identity cards, driving licenses or similar documents), account files and business correspondence for at least five years after the business relationship is ended.

The identification data and transaction records should be available to domestic competent authorities upon appropriate authority.

11.* Financial institutions should pay special attention to all complex, unusual large transactions, and all unusual patterns of transactions, which have no apparent economic or visible lawful purpose. The background and purpose of such transactions should, as far as possible, be examined; the findings should be established in writing, and available to help competent authorities and auditors.

12.* The customer due diligence and record-keeping requirements set out in Recommendations 5, 6, and 8 to 11 apply to designated non-financial businesses and professions in the following situations:

a) Casinos – when customers engage in financial transactions equal to or above the applicable designated threshold.

b) Real-estate agents – when they are involved in transactions for their client concerning the buying and selling of real estate.

c)   Dealers in precious metals and dealers in precious stones – when they engage in any cash transaction with a customer equal to or above the applicable designated threshold.

d)   Lawyers, notaries, other independent legal professionals and accountants when they prepare for or carry out transactions for their client concerning the following activities:

- buying and selling of real estate;

- managing of client money, securities or other assets;

- management of bank, savings or securities accounts;

- organisation of contributions for the creation, operation or management of companies;

- creation, operation or management of legal persons or arrangements, and buying and selling of business entities.

e)   Trust and company service providers when they prepare for or carry out transactions for a client concerning the activities listed in the definition in the Glossary.

Reporting of suspicious transactions and compliance

13.* If a financial institution suspects or has reasonable grounds to suspect that funds are the proceeds of a criminal activity, or are related to terrorist financing, it should be required, directly by law or regulation, to report promptly its suspicions to the financial intelligence unit (FIU).

14.* Financial institutions, their directors, officers and employees should be:

a)   Protected by legal provisions from criminal and civil liability for breach of any restriction on disclosure of information imposed by contract or by any legislative, regulatory or administrative provision, if they report their suspicions in good faith to the FIU, even if they did not know precisely what the underlying criminal activity was, and regardless of whether illegal activity actually occurred.

b)   Prohibited by law from disclosing the fact that a suspicious transaction report (STR) or related information is being reported to the FIU.

15.* Financial institutions should develop programmes against money laundering and terrorist financing. These programmes should include:

a)   The development of internal policies, procedures and controls, including appropriate compliance management arrangements, and adequate screening procedures to ensure high standards when hiring employees.

b)   An ongoing employee training programme.

c)   An audit function to test the system.

16.* The requirements set out in Recommendations 13 to 15, and 21 apply to all designated non-financial businesses and professions, subject to the following qualifications:

a)   Lawyers, notaries, other independent legal professionals and accountants should be required to report suspicious transactions when, on behalf of or for a client, they engage in a financial transaction in relation to the activities described in Recommendation 12(d). Countries are strongly encouraged to extend the reporting requirement to the rest of the professional activities of accountants, including auditing.

b)   Dealers in precious metals and dealers in precious stones should be required to report suspicious transactions when they engage in any cash transaction with a customer equal to or above the applicable designated threshold.

c)   Trust and company service providers should be required to report suspicious transactions for a client when, on behalf of or for a client, they engage in a transaction in relation to the activities referred to Recommendation 12(e).

Lawyers, notaries, other independent legal professionals, and accountants acting as independent legal professionals, are not required to report their suspicions if the relevant information was obtained in circumstances where they are subject to professional secrecy or legal professional privilege.

Other measures to deter money laundering and terrorist financing

17. Countries should ensure that effective, proportionate and dissuasive sanctions, whether criminal, civil or administrative, are available to deal with natural or legal persons covered by these Recommendations that fail to comply with anti-money laundering or terrorist financing requirements.

18. Countries should not approve the establishment or accept the continued operation of shell banks. Financial institutions should refuse to enter into, or continue, a correspondent banking relationship with shell banks. Financial institutions should also guard against establishing relations with respondent foreign financial institutions that permit their accounts to be used by shell banks.

19. Countries should consider the feasibility and utility of a system where banks and other financial institutions and intermediaries would report all domestic and international currency transactions above a fixed amount, to a national central agency with a computerised data base, available to competent authorities for use in money laundering or terrorist financing cases, subject to strict safeguards to ensure proper use of the information.

20. Countries should consider applying the FATF Recommendations to businesses and professions, other than designated non-financial businesses and professions, that pose a money laundering or terrorist financing risk. Countries should further encourage the development of modern and secure techniques of money management that are less vulnerable to money laundering.

Measures to be taken with respect to countries that do not or insufficiently comply with the FATF Recommendations

21. Financial institutions should give special attention to business relationships and transactions with persons, including companies and financial institutions, from countries which do not or insufficiently apply the FATF Recommendations. Whenever these transactions have no apparent economic or visible lawful purpose, their background and purpose should, as far as possible, be examined; the findings should be established in writing, and available to help competent authorities. Where such a country continues not to apply or insufficiently applies the FATF Recommendations, countries should be able to apply appropriate countermeasures.

22. Financial institutions should ensure that the principles applicable to financial institutions, which are mentioned above, are also applied to branches and majority owned subsidiaries located abroad, especially in countries which do not or insufficiently apply the FATF Recommendations, to the extent that local applicable laws and regulations permit. When local applicable laws and regulations prohibit this implementation, competent authorities in the country of the parent institution should be informed by the financial institutions that they cannot apply the FATF Recommendations.

Regulation and supervision

23.* Countries should ensure that financial institutions are subject to adequate regulation and supervision and are effectively implementing the FATF Recommendations. Competent authorities should take the necessary legal or regulatory measures to prevent criminals or their associates from holding or being the beneficial owner of a significant or controlling interest or holding a management function in a financial institution.

For financial institutions subject to the Core Principles, the regulatory and supervisory measures that apply for prudential purposes, and which are also relevant to money laundering, should apply in a similar manner for anti-money laundering and terrorist financing purposes.

Other financial institutions should be licensed or registered and appropriately regulated, and subject to supervision or oversight for anti-money laundering purposes, having regard to the risk of money laundering or terrorist financing in that sector. At a minimum, businesses providing a service of money or value transfer, or of money or currency changing should be licensed or registered, and subject to effective systems for monitoring and ensuring compliance with national requirements to combat money laundering and terrorist financing.

24. Designated non-financial businesses and professions should be subject to regulatory and supervisory measures as set out below.

a)   Casinos should be subject to a comprehensive regulatory and supervisory regime that ensures that they have effectively implemented the necessary anti-money laundering and terrorist-financing measures. At a minimum:

   • casinos should be licensed;

   • competent authorities should take the necessary legal or regulatory measures to prevent criminals or their associates from holding or being the beneficial owner of a significant or controlling interest, holding a management function in, or being an operator of a casino;

- competent authorities should ensure that casinos are effectively supervised for compliance with requirements to combat money laundering and terrorist financing.

b) Countries should ensure that the other categories of designated non-financial businesses and professions are subject to effective systems for monitoring and ensuring their compliance with requirements to combat money laundering and terrorist financing. This should be performed on a risk-sensitive basis. This may be performed by a government authority or by an appropriate self-regulatory organisation, provided that such an organisation can ensure that its members comply with their obligations to combat money laundering and terrorist financing.

25. * The competent authorities should establish guidelines, and provide feedback which will assist financial institutions and designated non-financial businesses and professions in applying national measures to combat money laundering and terrorist financing, and in particular, in detecting and reporting suspicious transactions.

C. INSTITUTIONAL AND OTHER MEASURES NECESSARY IN SYSTEMS FOR COMBATING MONEY LAUNDERING AND TERRORIST FINANCING

Competent authorities, their powers and resources

26. * Countries should establish a FIU that serves as a national centre for the receiving (and, as permitted, requesting), analysis and dissemination of STR and other information regarding potential money laundering or terrorist financing. The FIU should have access, directly or indirectly, on a timely basis to the financial, administrative and law enforcement information that it requires to properly undertake its functions, including the analysis of STR.

27. * Countries should ensure that designated law enforcement authorities have responsibility for money laundering and terrorist financing investigations. Countries are encouraged to support and develop, as far as possible, special investigative techniques suitable for the investigation of money laundering, such as controlled delivery, undercover operations and other relevant techniques. Countries are also encouraged to use other effective mechanisms such as the use of permanent or temporary groups specialised in asset investigation, and co-operative investigations with appropriate competent authorities in other countries.

28. When conducting investigations of money laundering and underlying predicate offences, competent authorities should be able to obtain documents and information for use in those investigations, and in prosecutions and related actions. This should include powers to use compulsory measures for the production of records held by financial institutions and other persons, for the search of persons and premises, and for the seizure and obtaining of evidence.

29. Supervisors should have adequate powers to monitor and ensure compliance by financial institutions with requirements to combat money laundering and terrorist financing, including the authority to conduct inspections. They should be authorised to compel production of any information from financial institutions that is relevant to monitoring such compliance, and to impose adequate administrative sanctions for failure to comply with such requirements.

30. Countries should provide their competent authorities involved in combating money laundering and terrorist financing with adequate financial, human and technical resources. Countries should have in place processes to ensure that the staff of those authorities are of high integrity.

31. Countries should ensure that policy makers, the FIU, law enforcement and supervisors have effective mechanisms in place which enable them to co-operate, and where appropriate coordinate domestically with each other concerning the development and implementation of policies and activities to combat money laundering and terrorist financing.

32. Countries should ensure that their competent authorities can review the effectiveness of their systems to combat money laundering and terrorist financing systems by maintaining comprehensive statistics on matters relevant to the effectiveness and efficiency of such systems. This should include statistics on the STR received and disseminated; on money laundering and terrorist financing investigations, prosecutions and convictions; on property frozen, seized and confiscated; and on mutual legal assistance or other international requests for co-operation.

Transparency of legal persons and arrangements

33. Countries should take measures to prevent the unlawful use of legal persons by money launderers. Countries should ensure that there is adequate, accurate and timely information on the beneficial ownership and control of legal persons that can be obtained or accessed in a timely fashion by competent authorities. In particular, countries that have legal persons that are able to issue bearer shares should take appropriate measures to ensure that they are not misused for money laundering and be able to demonstrate the adequacy of those measures. Countries could consider measures to facilitate access to beneficial ownership and control information to financial institutions undertaking the requirements set out in Recommendation 5.

34. Countries should take measures to prevent the unlawful use of legal arrangements by money launderers. In particular, countries should ensure that there is adequate, accurate and timely information on express trusts, including information on the settlor, trustee and beneficiaries, that can be obtained or accessed in a timely fashion by competent authorities. Countries could consider measures to facilitate access to beneficial ownership and control information to financial institutions undertaking the requirements set out in Recommendation 5.

D. INTERNATIONAL CO-OPERATION

35. Countries should take immediate steps to become party to and implement fully the Vienna Convention, the Palermo Convention, and the 1999 United Nations International Convention for the Suppression of the Financing of Terrorism. Countries are also encouraged to ratify and implement other relevant international conventions, such as the 1990 Council of Europe Convention on Laundering, Search, Seizure and Confiscation of the Proceeds from Crime and the 2002 Inter-American Convention against Terrorism.

Mutual legal assistance and extradition

36. Countries should rapidly, constructively and effectively provide the widest possible range of mutual legal assistance in relation to money laundering and terrorist financing investigations, prosecutions, and related proceedings. In particular, countries should:

a) Not prohibit or place unreasonable or unduly restrictive conditions on the provision of mutual legal assistance.

b) Ensure that they have clear and efficient processes for the execution of mutual legal assistance requests.

c) Not refuse to execute a request for mutual legal assistance on the sole ground that the offence is also considered to involve fiscal matters.

d) Not refuse to execute a request for mutual legal assistance on the grounds that laws require financial institutions to maintain secrecy or confidentiality.

Countries should ensure that the powers of their competent authorities required under Recommendation 28 are also available for use in response to requests for mutual legal assistance, and if consistent with their domestic framework, in response to direct requests from foreign judicial or law enforcement authorities to domestic counterparts.

To avoid conflicts of jurisdiction, consideration should be given to devising and applying mechanisms for determining the best venue for prosecution of defendants in the interests of justice in cases that are subject to prosecution in more than one country.

37. Countries should, to the greatest extent possible, render mutual legal assistance notwithstanding the absence of dual criminality.

Where dual criminality is required for mutual legal assistance or extradition, that requirement should be deemed to be satisfied regardless of whether both countries place the offence within the same category of offence or denominate the offence by the same terminology, provided that both countries criminalise the conduct underlying the offence.

38.* There should be authority to take expeditious action in response to requests by foreign countries to identify, freeze, seize and confiscate property laundered, proceeds from money laundering or predicate offences, instrumentalities used in or intended for use in the commission of these offences, or property of corresponding value. There should also be arrangements for co-ordinating seizure and confiscation proceedings, which may include the sharing of confiscated assets.

39. Countries should recognise money laundering as an extraditable offence. Each country should either extradite its own nationals, or where a country does not do so solely on the grounds of nationality, that country should, at the request of the country seeking extradition, submit the case without undue delay to its competent authorities for the purpose of prosecution of the offences set forth in the request. Those authorities should take their decision and conduct their proceedings in the same manner as in the case of any other offence of a serious nature under the domestic law of that country. The countries concerned should cooperate with each other, in particular on procedural and evidentiary aspects, to ensure the efficiency of such prosecutions.

Subject to their legal frameworks, countries may consider simplifying extradition by allowing direct transmission of extradition requests between appropriate ministries, extraditing persons based only on warrants of arrests or judgements, and/or introducing a simplified extradition of consenting persons who waive formal extradition proceedings.

Other forms of co-operation

40.* Countries should ensure that their competent authorities provide the widest possible range of international co-operation to their foreign counterparts. There should be clear and effective gateways to facilitate the prompt and constructive exchange directly between counterparts, either spontaneously or upon request, of information relating to both money laundering and the underlying predicate offences. Exchanges should be permitted without unduly restrictive conditions. In particular:

    a)   Competent authorities should not refuse a request for assistance on the sole ground that the request is also considered to involve fiscal matters.

    b)   Countries should not invoke laws that require financial institutions to maintain secrecy or confidentiality as a ground for refusing to provide co-operation.

    c)   Competent authorities should be able to conduct inquiries – and where possible, investigations – on behalf of foreign counterparts.

Where the ability to obtain information sought by a foreign competent authority is not within the mandate of its counterpart, countries are also encouraged to permit a prompt and constructive exchange of information with non-counterparts. Co-operation with foreign authorities other than counterparts could occur directly or indirectly. When uncertain about the appropriate avenue to follow, competent authorities should first contact their foreign counterparts for assistance.

Countries should establish controls and safeguards to ensure that information exchanged by competent authorities is used only in an authorised manner, consistent with their obligations concerning privacy and data protection.

GLOSSARY

In these Recommendations the following abbreviations and references are used:

'**Beneficial owner**' refers to the natural person(s) who ultimately owns or controls a customer and/or the person on whose behalf a transaction is being conducted. It also incorporates those persons who exercise ultimate effective control over a legal person or arrangement.

'**Core Principles**' refers to the Core Principles for Effective Banking Supervision issued by the Basel Committee on Banking Supervision, the Objectives and Principles for Securities Regulation issued by the International Organization of Securities Commissions, and the Insurance Supervisory Principles issued by the International Association of Insurance Supervisors.

'**Designated categories of offences**' means:

- participation in an organised criminal group and racketeering;
- terrorism, including terrorist financing;
- trafficking in human beings and migrant smuggling;
- sexual exploitation, including sexual exploitation of children;
- illicit trafficking in narcotic drugs and psychotropic substances;
- illicit arms trafficking;
- illicit trafficking in stolen and other goods;
- corruption and bribery;
- fraud;
- counterfeiting currency;
- counterfeiting and piracy of products;
- environmental crime;
- murder, grievous bodily injury;
- kidnapping, illegal restraint and hostage-taking;
- robbery or theft;
- smuggling;

- extortion;

- forgery;

- piracy; and

- insider trading and market manipulation.

When deciding on the range of offences to be covered as predicate offences under each of the categories listed above, each country may decide, in accordance with its domestic law, how it will define those offences and the nature of any particular elements of those offences that make them serious offences.

'Designated non-financial businesses and professions' means:

a) Casinos (which also includes Internet casinos).

b) Real-estate agents.

c) Dealers in precious metals.

d) Dealers in precious stones.

e) Lawyers, notaries, other independent legal professionals and accountants – this refers to sole practitioners, partners or employed professionals within professional firms. It is not meant to refer to 'internal' professionals that are employees of other types of businesses, nor to professionals working for government agencies, who may already be subject to measures that would combat money laundering.

f) Trust and company service providers – this refers to all persons or businesses that are not covered elsewhere under these Recommendations, and which, as a business, provide any of the following services to third parties:

  - acting as a formation agent of legal persons;

  - acting as (or arranging for another person to act as) a director or secretary of a company, a partner of a partnership, or a similar position in relation to other legal persons;

  - providing a registered office; business address or accommodation, correspondence or administrative address for a company, a partnership or any other legal person or arrangement;

- acting as (or arranging for another person to act as) a trustee of an express trust;

- acting as (or arranging for another person to act as) a nominee shareholder for another person.

'Designated threshold' refers to the amount set out in the Interpretative Notes.

'Financial institutions' means any person or entity who conducts as a business one or more of the following activities or operations for or on behalf of a customer:

1. Acceptance of deposits and other repayable funds from the public.[5]

2. Lending.[6]

3. Financial leasing.[7]

4. The transfer of money or value.[8]

5. Issuing and managing means of payment (for example, credit and debit cards, cheques, traveller's cheques, money orders and bankers' drafts, electronic money).

6. Financial guarantees and commitments.

7. Trading in:

    (a) money market instruments (cheques, bills, CDs, derivatives, and so on);

    (b) foreign exchange;

    (c) exchange, interest rate and index instruments;

    (d) transferable securities;

    (e) commodity futures trading.

---

5   This also captures private banking.
6   This includes, *inter alia*, consumer credit; mortgage credit; factoring, with or without recourse; and finance of commercial transactions (including forfeiting).
7   This does not extend to financial leasing arrangements in relation to consumer products.
8   This applies to financial activity in both the formal or informal sector, for example alternative remittance activity. See the Interpretative Note to Special Recommendation VI. It does not apply to any natural or legal person that provides financial institutions solely with message or other support systems for transmitting funds. See the Interpretative Note to Special Recommendation VII.

8.   Participation in securities issues and the provision of financial services related to such issues.

9.   Individual and collective portfolio management.

10.   Safekeeping and administration of cash or liquid securities on behalf of other persons.

11.   Otherwise investing, administering or managing funds or money on behalf of other persons.

12.   Underwriting and placement of life insurance and other investment related insurance.[9]

13.   Money and currency changing.

14.   When a financial activity is carried out by a person or entity on an occasional or very limited basis (having regard to quantitative and absolute criteria) such that there is little risk of money laundering activity occurring, a country may decide that the application of anti-money laundering measures is not necessary, either fully or partially. In strictly limited and justified circumstances, and based on a proven low risk of money laundering, a country may decide not to apply some or all of the Forty Recommendations to some of the financial activities stated above.

'**FIU**' means financial intelligence unit.

'**Legal arrangements**' refers to express trusts or other similar legal arrangements.

'**Legal persons**' refers to bodies corporate, foundations, anstalt, partnerships, or associations, or any similar bodies that can establish a permanent customer relationship with a financial institution or otherwise own property.

'**Payable-through accounts**' refers to correspondent accounts that are used directly by third parties to transact business on their own behalf.

'**Politically exposed persons**' (PEPs) are individuals who are or have been entrusted with prominent public functions in a foreign country, for example Heads of State or of government, senior politicians, senior government, judicial or military officials, senior executives of state owned corporations, important

---

9   This applies both to insurance undertakings and to insurance intermediaries (agents and brokers).

political party officials. Business relationships with family members or close associates of PEPs involve reputational risks similar to those with PEPs themselves. The definition is not intended to cover middle ranking or more junior individuals in the foregoing categories.

'Shell bank' means a bank incorporated in a jurisdiction in which it has no physical presence and which is unaffiliated with a regulated financial group.

'STR' refers to suspicious transaction reports.

'Supervisors' refers to the designated competent authorities responsible for ensuring compliance by financial institutions with requirements to combat money laundering and terrorist financing.

'The FATF Recommendations' refers to these Recommendations and to the FATF Special Recommendations on Terrorist Financing.

ANNEX: INTERPRETATIVE NOTES TO THE FORTY RECOMMENDATIONS

INTERPRETATIVE NOTES

General

1. Reference in this document to 'countries' should be taken to apply equally to 'territories' or 'jurisdictions'.

2. Recommendations 5–16 and 21–22 state that financial institutions or designated non-financial businesses and professions should take certain actions. These references require countries to take measures that will oblige financial institutions or designated non-financial businesses and professions to comply with each Recommendation. The basic obligations under Recommendations 5, 10 and 13 should be set out in law or regulation, while more detailed elements in those Recommendations, as well as obligations under other Recommendations, could be required either by law or regulation or by other enforceable means issued by a competent authority.

3. Where reference is made to a financial institution being satisfied as to a matter, that institution must be able to justify its assessment to competent authorities.

4. To comply with Recommendations 12 and 16, countries do not need to issue laws or regulations that relate exclusively to lawyers, notaries, accountants and the other designated non-financial businesses and professions so long as these businesses or professions are included in laws or regulations covering the underlying activities.

5. The Interpretative Notes that apply to financial institutions are also relevant to designated non-financial businesses and professions, where applicable.

Recommendations 5, 12 and 16

The designated thresholds for transactions (under Recommendations 5 and 12) are as follows:

- Financial institutions (for occasional customers under Recommendation 5) – USD/EUR 15 000.

- Casinos, including internet casinos (under Recommendation 12) – USD/EUR 3000.

- For dealers in precious metals and dealers in precious stones when engaged in any cash transaction (under Recommendations 12 and 16) – USD/EUR 15 000.

Financial transactions above a designated threshold include situations where the transaction is carried out in a single operation or in several operations that appear to be linked.

RECOMMENDATION 5

Customer due diligence and tipping off

1. If, during the establishment or course of the customer relationship, or when conducting occasional transactions, a financial institution suspects that transactions relate to money laundering or terrorist financing, then the institution should:

   a)   Normally seek to identify and verify the identity of the customer and the beneficial owner, whether permanent or occasional, and irrespective of any exemption or any designated threshold that might otherwise apply.

   b)   Make a STR to the FIU in accordance with Recommendation 13.

2. Recommendation 14 prohibits financial institutions, their directors, officers and employees from disclosing the fact that an STR or related information is being reported to the FIU. A risk exists that customers could be unintentionally tipped off when the financial institution is seeking to perform its customer due diligence (CDD) obligations in these circumstances. The customer's awareness of a possible STR or investigation could compromise future efforts to investigate the suspected money laundering or terrorist financing operation.

3. Therefore, if financial institutions form a suspicion that transactions relate to money laundering or terrorist financing, they should take into account the risk of tipping off when performing the customer due diligence process. If the institution reasonably believes that performing the CDD process will tip-off the customer or potential customer, it may choose not to pursue that process, and should file an STR. Institutions should ensure that their employees are aware of and sensitive to these issues when conducting CDD.

CDD for legal persons and arrangements

4. When performing elements (a) and (b) of the CDD process in relation to legal persons or arrangements, financial institutions should:

a) Verify that any person purporting to act on behalf of the customer is so authorised, and identify that person.

b) Identify the customer and verify their identity – the types of measures that would be normally needed to satisfactorily perform this function would require obtaining proof of incorporation or similar evidence of the legal status of the legal person or arrangement, as well as information concerning the customer's name, the names of trustees, legal form, address, directors, and provisions regulating the power to bind the legal person or arrangement.

c) Identify the beneficial owners, including forming an understanding of the ownership and control structure, and take reasonable measures to verify the identity of such persons. The types of measures that would be normally needed to satisfactorily perform this function would require identifying the natural persons with a controlling interest and identifying the natural persons who comprise the mind and management of the legal person or arrangement. Where the customer or the owner of the controlling interest is a public company that is subject to regulatory disclosure requirements, it is not necessary to seek to identify and verify the identity of any shareholder of that company.

The relevant information or data may be obtained from a public register, from the customer or from other reliable sources.

Reliance on identification and verification already performed

5. The CDD measures set out in Recommendation 5 do not imply that financial institutions have to repeatedly identify and verify the identity of each customer every time that a customer conducts a transaction. An institution is entitled to rely on the identification and verification steps that it has already undertaken unless it has doubts about the veracity of that information.

Examples of situations that might lead an institution to have such doubts could be where there is a suspicion of money laundering in relation to that customer, or where there is a material change in the way that the customer's account is operated which is not consistent with the customer's business profile.

Timing of verification

6. Examples of the types of circumstances where it would be permissible for verification to be completed after the establishment of the business relationship, because it would be essential not to interrupt the normal conduct of business include:

- Non face-to-face business.

- Securities transactions. In the securities industry, companies and intermediaries may be required to perform transactions very rapidly, according to the market conditions at the time the customer is contacting them, and the performance of the transaction may be required before verification of identity is completed.

- Life insurance business. In relation to life insurance business, countries may permit the identification and verification of the beneficiary under the policy to take place after having established the business relationship with the policyholder. However, in all such cases, identification and verification should occur at or before the time of payout or the time where the beneficiary intends to exercise vested rights under the policy.

7. Financial institutions will also need to adopt risk management procedures with respect to the conditions under which a customer may utilise the business relationship prior to verification. These procedures should include a set of measures such as a limitation of the number, types and/or amount of transactions that can be performed and the monitoring of large or complex transactions being carried out outside of expected norms for that type of relationship. Financial institutions should refer to the Basel CDD paper[10] (section 2.2.6.) for specific guidance on examples of risk management measures for non-face-to-face business.

Requirement to identify existing customers

8. The principles set out in the Basel CDD paper concerning the identification of existing customers should serve as guidance when applying customer due

---

10 'Basel CDD paper' refers to the guidance paper on Customer Due Diligence for Banks issued by the Basel Committee on Banking Supervision in October 2001.

diligence processes to institutions engaged in banking activity, and could apply to other financial institutions where relevant.

Simplified or reduced CDD measures

9. The general rule is that customers must be subject to the full range of CDD measures, including the requirement to identify the beneficial owner. Nevertheless there are circumstances where the risk of money laundering or terrorist financing is lower, where information on the identity of the customer and the beneficial owner of a customer is publicly available, or where adequate checks and controls exist elsewhere in national systems. In such circumstances it could be reasonable for a country to allow its financial institutions to apply simplified or reduced CDD measures when identifying and verifying the identity of the customer and the beneficial owner.

10. Examples of customers where simplified or reduced CDD measures could apply are:

- Financial institutions – where they are subject to requirements to combat money laundering and terrorist financing consistent with the FATF Recommendations and are supervised for compliance with those controls.

- Public companies that are subject to regulatory disclosure requirements.

- Government administrations or enterprises.

11. Simplified or reduced CDD measures could also apply to the beneficial owners of pooled accounts held by designated non-financial businesses or professions provided that those businesses or professions are subject to requirements to combat money laundering and terrorist financing consistent with the FATF Recommendations and are subject to effective systems for monitoring and ensuring their compliance with those requirements. Banks should also refer to the Basel CDD paper (section 2.2.4.), which provides specific guidance concerning situations where an account-holding institution may rely on a customer that is a professional financial intermediary to perform the customer due diligence on his or its own customers (that is, the beneficial owners of the bank account). Where relevant, the CDD paper could also provide guidance in relation to similar accounts held by other types of financial institutions.

12. Simplified CDD or reduced measures could also be acceptable for various types of products or transactions such as (examples only):

- Life insurance policies where the annual premium is no more than USD/EUR 1000 or single premium is no more than USD/EUR 2500.

- Insurance policies for pension schemes if there is no surrender clause and the policy cannot be used as collateral.

- A pension, superannuation or similar scheme that provides retirement benefits to employees, where contributions are made by way of deduction from wages and the scheme rules do not permit the assignment of a member's interest under the scheme.

13. Countries could also decide whether financial institutions could apply these simplified measures only to customers in its own jurisdiction or allow them to do for customers from any other jurisdiction that the original country is satisfied is in compliance with and has effectively implemented the FATF Recommendations.

Simplified CDD measures are not acceptable whenever there is suspicion of money laundering or terrorist financing or specific higher risk scenarios apply.

Recommendation 6

Countries are encouraged to extend the requirements of Recommendation 6 to individuals who hold prominent public functions in their own country.

Recommendation 9

This Recommendation does not apply to outsourcing or agency relationships.

This Recommendation also does not apply to relationships, accounts or transactions between financial institutions for their clients. Those relationships are addressed by Recommendations 5 and 7.

Recommendations 10 and 11

In relation to insurance business, the word 'transactions' should be understood to refer to the insurance product itself, the premium payment and the benefits.

Recommendation 13

1. The reference to criminal activity in Recommendation 13 refers to:

   a)   all criminal acts that would constitute a predicate offence for money laundering in the jurisdiction; or

b) at a minimum to those offences that would constitute a predicate offence as required by Recommendation 1.

Countries are strongly encouraged to adopt alternative (a). All suspicious transactions, including attempted transactions, should be reported regardless of the amount of the transaction.

2. In implementing Recommendation 13, suspicious transactions should be reported by financial institutions regardless of whether they are also thought to involve tax matters. Countries should take into account that, in order to deter financial institutions from reporting a suspicious transaction, money launderers may seek to state *inter alia* that their transactions relate to tax matters.

Recommendation 14 (tipping off)

Where lawyers, notaries, other independent legal professionals and accountants acting as independent legal professionals seek to dissuade a client from engaging in illegal activity, this does not amount to tipping off.

Recommendation 15

The type and extent of measures to be taken for each of the requirements set out in the Recommendations should be appropriate having regard to the risk of money laundering and terrorist financing and the size of the business.

For financial institutions, compliance management arrangements should include the appointment of a compliance officer at the management level.

Recommendation 16

1. It is for each jurisdiction to determine the matters that would fall under legal professional privilege or professional secrecy. This would normally cover information lawyers, notaries or other independent legal professionals receive from or obtain through one of their clients: (a) in the course of ascertaining the legal position of their client, or (b) in performing their task of defending or representing that client in, or concerning judicial, administrative, arbitration or mediation proceedings. Where accountants are subject to the same obligations of secrecy or privilege, then they are also not required to report suspicious transactions.

2. Countries may allow lawyers, notaries, other independent legal professionals and accountants to send their STR to their appropriate self-regulatory organisations, provided that there are appropriate forms of co-operation between these organisations and the FIU.

Recommendation 23

Recommendation 23 should not be read as to require the introduction of a system of regular review of licensing of controlling interests in financial institutions merely for anti-money laundering purposes, but as to stress the desirability of suitability review for controlling shareholders in financial institutions (banks and non-banks in particular) from a FATF point of view. Hence, where shareholder suitability (or 'fit and proper') tests exist, the attention of supervisors should be drawn to their relevance for anti-money laundering purposes.

Recommendation 25

When considering the feedback that should be provided, countries should have regard to the FATF Best Practice Guidelines on Providing Feedback to Reporting Financial Institutions and Other Persons.

Recommendation 26

Where a country has created an FIU, it should consider applying for membership in the Egmont Group. Countries should have regard to the Egmont Group Statement of Purpose, and its Principles for Information Exchange Between Financial Intelligence Units for Money Laundering Cases. These documents set out important guidance concerning the role and functions of FIUs, and the mechanisms for exchanging information between FIUs.

Recommendation 27

Countries should consider taking measures, including legislative ones, at the national level, to allow their competent authorities investigating money laundering cases to postpone or waive the arrest of suspected persons and/ or the seizure of the money for the purpose of identifying persons involved in such activities or for evidence gathering. Without such measures the use of procedures such as controlled deliveries and undercover operations are precluded.

Recommendation 38

Countries should consider:

a) Establishing an asset forfeiture fund in its respective country into which all or a portion of confiscated property will be deposited for law enforcement, health, education, or other appropriate purposes.

b) Taking such measures as may be necessary to enable it to share among or between other countries confiscated property, in particular, when confiscation is directly or indirectly a result of co-ordinated law enforcement actions.

Recommendation 40

1. For the purposes of this Recommendation:

- 'Counterparts' refers to authorities that exercise similar responsibilities and functions.

- 'Competent authority' refers to all administrative and law enforcement authorities concerned with combating money laundering and terrorist financing, including the FIU and supervisors.

2. Depending on the type of competent authority involved and the nature and purpose of the co-operation, different channels can be appropriate for the exchange of information. Examples of mechanisms or channels that are used to exchange information include: bilateral or multilateral agreements or arrangements, memoranda of understanding, exchanges on the basis of reciprocity, or through appropriate international or regional organisations. However, this Recommendation is not intended to cover co-operation in relation to mutual legal assistance or extradition.

3. The reference to indirect exchange of information with foreign authorities other than counterparts covers the situation where the requested information passes from the foreign authority through one or more domestic or foreign authorities before being received by the requesting authority. The competent authority that requests the information should always make it clear for what purpose and on whose behalf the request is made.

4. FIUs should be able to make inquiries on behalf of foreign counterparts where this could be relevant to an analysis of financial transactions. At a minimum, inquiries should include:

- Searching its own databases, which would include information related to suspicious transaction reports.

- Searching other databases to which it may have direct or indirect access, including law enforcement databases, public databases, administrative databases and commercially available databases.

Where permitted to do so, FIUs should also contact other competent authorities and financial institutions in order to obtain relevant information.

Special Recommendations on Terrorist Financing

Financial Action Task Force on Money Laundering/ Group d'action financière sur le blanchiment de capiteaux (FATF/GAFI)

Recognising the vital importance of taking action to combat the financing of terrorism, the FATF has agreed these Recommendations, which, when combined with the FATF Forty Recommendations on money laundering, set out the basic framework to detect, prevent and suppress the financing of terrorism and terrorist acts.

I. RATIFICATION AND IMPLEMENTATION OF UN INSTRUMENTS

Each country should take immediate steps to ratify and to implement fully the 1999 United Nations International Convention for the Suppression of the Financing of Terrorism.

Countries should also immediately implement the United Nations resolutions relating to the prevention and suppression of the financing of terrorist acts, particularly United Nations Security Council Resolution 1373.

II. CRIMINALISING THE FINANCING OF TERRORISM AND ASSOCIATED MONEY LAUNDERING

Each country should criminalise the financing of terrorism, terrorist acts and terrorist organisations. Countries should ensure that such offences are designated as money laundering predicate offences.

III. FREEZING AND CONFISCATING TERRORIST ASSETS

Each country should implement measures to freeze without delay funds or other assets of terrorists, those who finance terrorism and terrorist organisations in accordance with the United Nations resolutions relating to the prevention and suppression of the financing of terrorist acts.

Each country should also adopt and implement measures, including legislative ones, which would enable the competent authorities to seize and confiscate property that is the proceeds of, or used in, or intended or allocated for use in, the financing of terrorism, terrorist acts or terrorist organisations.

IV. REPORTING SUSPICIOUS TRANSACTIONS RELATED TO TERRORISM

If financial institutions, or other businesses or entities subject to anti-money laundering obligations, suspect or have reasonable grounds to suspect that funds are linked or related to, or are to be used for, terrorism, terrorist acts or by terrorist organisations, they should be required to report promptly their suspicions to the competent authorities.

V. INTERNATIONAL CO-OPERATION

Each country should afford another country, on the basis of a treaty, arrangement or other mechanism for mutual legal assistance or information exchange, the greatest possible measure of assistance in connection with criminal, civil enforcement, and administrative investigations, inquiries and proceedings relating to the financing of terrorism, terrorist acts and terrorist organisations.

Countries should also take all possible measures to ensure that they do not provide safe havens for individuals charged with the financing of terrorism, terrorist acts or terrorist organisations, and should have procedures in place to extradite, where possible, such individuals.

VI. ALTERNATIVE REMITTANCE

Each country should take measures to ensure that persons or legal entities, including agents, that provide a service for the transmission of money or value, including transmission through an informal money or value transfer system or network, should be licensed or registered and subject to all the FATF Recommendations that apply to banks and non-bank financial institutions. Each country should ensure that persons or legal entities that carry out this service illegally are subject to administrative, civil or criminal sanctions.

VII. WIRE TRANSFERS

Countries should take measures to require financial institutions, including money remitters, to include accurate and meaningful originator information (name, address and account number) on funds transfers and related messages that are sent, and the information should remain with the transfer or related message through the payment chain.

Countries should take measures to ensure that financial institutions, including money remitters, conduct enhanced scrutiny of and monitor for suspicious activity funds transfers which do not contain complete originator information (name, address and account number).

VIII. NON-PROFIT ORGANISATIONS

Countries should review the adequacy of laws and regulations that relate to entities that can be abused for the financing of terrorism. Non-profit organisations are particularly vulnerable, and countries should ensure that they cannot be misused:

(i)   by terrorist organisations posing as legitimate entities;

(ii)   to exploit legitimate entities as conduits for terrorist financing, including for the purpose of escaping asset-freezing measures; and

(iii)   to conceal or obscure the clandestine diversion of funds intended for legitimate purposes to terrorist organisations.

IX. CASH COURIERS

Countries should have measures in place to detect the physical cross-border transportation of currency and bearer negotiable instruments, including a declaration system or other disclosure obligation.

Countries should ensure that their competent authorities have the legal authority to stop or restrain currency or bearer negotiable instruments that are suspected to be related to terrorist financing or money laundering, or that are falsely declared or disclosed.

Countries should ensure that effective, proportionate and dissuasive sanctions are available to deal with persons who make false declaration(s) or disclosure(s). In cases where the currency or bearer negotiable instruments are related to terrorist financing or money laundering, countries should also adopt measures, including legislative ones consistent with Recommendation 3 and Special Recommendation III, which would enable the confiscation of such currency or instruments.

Index

About the Author

Doug Hopton is a consultant on financial crime prevention operating through his own company, DTH Associates Ltd. Before establishing his company in January 2003, he was with Barclays Bank for over 37 years, for many of which he was Head of Group Fraud and Money Laundering Prevention.

In this position he was responsible for the day-to-day coordination, monitoring, investigation and prevention of fraud against the Barclays Group worldwide. He was also responsible for the Bank's worldwide compliance with anti-money laundering legislation and, as Money Laundering Reporting Officer for the Barclays Group, he was the approved person under the Financial Services Authority rules.

Externally, he was a member of the former HM Treasury Money Laundering Experts Group, chairman of the Mainstream Banking Advisory Panel of the UK Joint Money Laundering Steering Group, and a member of the Financial Services Authority Rule Book Advisory Panel.

The author speaks widely on all aspects of financial crime prevention and has contributed to a number of books and articles on money laundering and fraud.

About DTH Associates

DTH Associates Ltd is a UK company specialising in the area of the prevention of financial crime, fraud and money laundering. This is provided by consultants who have had many years of practical experience in the industry before moving into consultancy. This ensures both a sound practical and theoretical solution is provided.

DTH Associates Ltd was established by Doug Hopton in 2003, prior to which he had many years of practical experience in a major international banking group where he headed up their Fraud and Money Laundering department. During his time with the bank he also sat on numerous industry and governmental committees and working parties.

Nothing has more exposed the vulnerability of systems, the weakness of inefficiently applied 'know your customer' rules, the lack of diligence in correspondent banking and the severe lack of information-sharing between different sectors and institutions, than 11 September 2001.

Private banks and insurance companies are in the front line in the resistance against financial fraud and financial crime. Organised crime and sophisticated terrorist networks exploit weak systems, personnel and inferior technology. In addition, ineffective regulation and toothless legislation have impeded governments and regulators alike and only now are institutions beginning to work much more closely together and help to create a common and effective collaborative framework.

Whether you are investigating complex, international organised fraud or local opportunist activities, your biggest challenges will be to manage and understand your data, highlight the nature and extent of your problem, and identify potential suspects. Whatever your investigative and analytical requirements, DTH Associates Ltd can help you.

FRAUD AND FINANCIAL CRIME PREVENTION

DTH Associates Ltd can deliver systems reviews, guidance and advice on the prevention of fraud and other financial crime as well as training services that are both practical and tailored to the specific needs of each client. They cover:

- Review of policies and procedures to assess compliance and an audit of their effectiveness.

- Awareness and training to meet your specific needs.

- Investigations into particular problems/losses.

A confidential exploratory discussion and evaluation of your needs can be arranged without a fee or further obligation.

INTERNAL FRAUD INVESTIGATIONS

DTH Associates Ltd can provide advice or assistance in the undertaking of internal investigations into suspected fraud or other losses. A review of systems and procedures to prevent future occurrences can be included in such advice.

ANTI-MONEY LAUNDERING COMPLIANCE PROCEDURES AND TRAINING

DTH Associates Ltd can deliver anti-money laundering compliance and training services that are both practical and tailored to the specific needs of each client. This would cover:

- Reviews of policies and procedures and an audit of their effectiveness and compliance against the appropriate legislation/regulations.

- Awareness and training to meet your specific needs.

- Confidential exploratory discussion and evaluation of your needs without a fee or further obligation.

DTH Associates Ltd can provide a solution worldwide, whether in the public or private sector.

Join our e-mail newsletter

Gower is widely recognized as one of the
world's leading publishers on management
and business practice. Its programmes
range from 1000-page handbooks through
practical manuals to popular paperbacks.
These cover all the main functions of
management: human resource development,
sales and marketing, project management,
finance, etc. Gower also produces
training videos and activities manuals on
a wide range of management skills.

As our list is constantly developing you
may find it difficult to keep abreast of new
titles. With this in mind we offer a free e-
mail news service, approximately once
every two months, which provides a brief
overview of the most recent titles and
links into our catalogue, should you wish
to read more or see sample pages.

To sign up to this service, send your request
via e-mail to info@gowerpub.com. Please
put your e-mail address in the body of the
e-mail as confirmation of your agreement
to receive information in this way.

GOWER